How We Win

I0125789

This book uniquely demonstrates how a new combination of communities, progressive visions, and strategies provides a path to defeat fascist machinations and strengthens social justice movements. Taking the incredible twists and turns of elections as a given, the book takes the issues, grievances and solutions of social movements as its grounding.

Would-be change agents, be they first-time voters, freshly minted activists, impacted communities, or veteran strategists, will find answers to questions of voting, organizing, and mobilization. In doing so, readers will find answers to activating their networks and communities not merely to vote, but how to build on their "Emergency Election" mobilizing and power-building efforts to win their agendas, regardless of who holds office.

This theoretically and empirically informed handbook for activists, voters, their organizations, unions, and communities provides both mobilizing tools and talking points about the elections' most vital and contested issues.

Charles Derber is professor of sociology at Boston College, USA. A lifelong social justice activist, his work focuses on the crises of capitalism, globalization, corporate power, militarism, the culture of hegemony, the climate crisis, and peace and global justice movements. His recent books include *Turnout!: Mobilizing Voters in an Emergency* (Routledge, 2020), *Dying for Capitalism: How Big Money Fuels Extinction and What We Can Do about It* (Routledge, 2023), and *Who Owns Democracy?: The Real Deep State and the Struggle over Class and Caste in America* (Routledge, 2024).

Suren Moodliar is an organizer, writer, and journal editor. He co-leads encuentro5, a Boston-based movement-building center. His most recent book is *Dying for Capitalism: How Big Money Fuels Extinction and What We Can Do about It* (Routledge, 2023).

Matt Nelson is executive director of Presente.org, an advocacy group that advances Latinx power and amplifies Latinx voices. Before his work at Presente.org, he was the organizing director at Color of Change. Matt is a seasoned campaign strategist, who has won dozens of local and national campaigns, and a skilled community organizer, who has trained thousands of activists. He is the co-editor of *Turnout!: Mobilizing Voters in an Emergency* (Routledge, 2020) and was featured in *Ferguson Is America: Roots of Rebellion* (2015).

Nancy Treviño is director of power at Presente.org, a community organizer, trainer, and campaign strategist. Previously, Nancy worked alongside dozens of grassroots community organizations across the US, collaborated with national and international human rights organizations, and continues to provide strategic organizing, digital, and communications support to advance social justice movements.

Universalizing Resistance Series
Edited by Charles Derber and Suren Moodliar

The modern social sciences began in the late 19th century when capitalism was establishing itself as the dominant global system. Social science began as a terrifying awakening: that a militarized, globalizing capitalism was creating the greatest revolution in history, penetrating every part of society with the passions of self-interest and profit and breaking down community and the common good. The universalizing of the market promised universal prosperity but delivered an intertwined sociopathic system of money-making, militarism and environmental destruction now threatening the survival of all life itself.

In the 21st century, only a universalized resistance to this now fully universalized matrix of money, militarism and me-firstism can save humanity. History shows that people can join together under nearly impossible odds to create movements against tyranny for the common good. But when the world faces a universalizing system of madness and extinction, it takes new forms of resistance moving Copyright Material – Provided by Taylor & Francis beyond the "silo" movements for social justice that have emerged notably in the US in recent decades: single-issue movements separated by issue, race, gender, social class, nation and geography. The story of what universalized movements look like, how they are beginning to be organized, how they "intersect" with each other against the reigning system of power, and how they can grow fast enough to save humanity is the purpose of this series.

The series is publishing works by leading thinkers and activists developing the theory and practice of universalizing resistance. The books are written to engage professors, students, activists and organizers, and citizens who recognize the desperate urgency of a universalizing resistance that can mobilize the general population to build a new global society preserving life with justice.

Forthcoming:

Disrupting Narratives of Deservedness: Changing the Stories that Hold Economic and Racial and Inequality in Place
Chuck Collins

Revolution Has an Address! The Transformative Power of Movement Building Spaces
Suren Moodliar

For more information about this series, please visit:
https://www.routledge.com/Universalizing-Resistance/book-series/RESIST

How We Win
Energizing Strategies, Voters, and Agendas

Edited by Charles Derber, Suren Moodliar, Matt Nelson, and Nancy Treviño

Routledge
Taylor & Francis Group

NEW YORK AND LONDON

First published 2025
by Routledge
605 Third Avenue, New York, NY 10158

and by Routledge
4 Park Square, Milton Park, Abingdon, Oxon, OX14 4RN

Routledge is an imprint of the Taylor & Francis Group, an informa business

© 2025 selection and editorial matter, Charles Derber, Suren
Moodliar, Matt Nelson and Nancy Treviño; individual
chapters, the contributors

The right of Charles Derber, Suren Moodliar, Matt Nelson
and Nancy Treviño to be identified as the authors of the
editorial material, and of the authors for their individual
chapters, has been asserted in accordance with sections 77
and 78 of the Copyright, Designs and Patents Act 1988.

All rights reserved. No part of this book may be reprinted
or reproduced or utilised in any form or by any electronic,
mechanical, or other means, now known or hereafter
invented, including photocopying and recording, or in any
information storage or retrieval system, without permission
in writing from the publishers.

Trademark notice: Product or corporate names may be
trademarks or registered trademarks, and are used only for
identification and explanation without intent to infringe.

ISBN: 978-1-032-89742-4 (hbk)
ISBN: 978-1-032-89741-7 (pbk)
ISBN: 978-1-003-54437-1 (ebk)

DOI: 10.4324/9781003544371

Typeset in Times New Roman
by Deanta Global Publishing Services, Chennai, India

Access the online chapters: www.routledge.com/
9781032897417 and www.emergencyelection.org/hww

Contents

Online Chapters

The below chapters can be accessed for free online at www.routledge.com/9781032897417 and www.emergencyelection.org/hww.

Acknowledgments

Elections are full of unexpected events and surprises, often encapsulated by the term "October Surprise" in the United States. These last-minute twists can shape the outcomes in unforeseen ways. Even in races where the results seem certain, the mood of the electorate, the morale of the base, and the candidates' demeanor assume outsized attention and weight, and can significantly influence the final outcome. The editors are therefore especially grateful to our many contributors for identifying and elaborating upon the foundational issues that constitute the bricks and mortar of the electoral path.

As the Democrats have passed the torch to a new generation of standard bearers and the MAGA Republicans advance their agenda of unfreedom, these foundational concerns — the increasingly assertive presence of the labor movement in our body politic, the expanded defense of bodily autonomy by women and their allies, climate breakdown and the policies that protect communities, environmental justices and related matters of housing and employment — are wending their way in national debate and campaign strategies. The effort of our contributors to share their perspective even as they are actively engaged in these battles is truly inspiring. Their insights and commitment are the very essence of our collective efforts to navigate the path ahead.

We extend our deepest gratitude to the countless individuals who have demonstrated the extraordinary power and dedication needed to advance our freedoms and shape our democracy. Our heartfelt thanks go out to each and every one of the contributors, friends, family members, and the incredible team at Routledge whose generous assistance and collective brilliance made this book possible. Your commitment to democracy and freedom is an inspiration to us all.

Throughout this book, organizational affiliations are listed for identification purposes only, and the authors are writing in their personal capacity.

Introduction

1 At the Crossroads, Again

Embracing Organizing, Social Movements, and Transformational Change

Charles Derber, Suren Moodliar, Matt Nelson and Nancy Treviño

Our elections have reached a boiling point: ballots mix with bullets, billions, and the bizarre, all while both major parties rapidly reintroduce themselves to the U.S. electorate. This is the emergency election of 2024. Strange brew notwithstanding, voters have crucial choices to make, including the solemn one in the ballot box. If their choices have rational footings, it is because the contributors to this volume and their allies have spotlighted the fundamental concerns of our time.

Voters in the United States, under increasing global public scrutiny, are once again facing an emergency election – that is, an election whose consequences go beyond politics and factor into the existential challenges of our day. These include extreme and extractive inequalities subsuming racial, gender, and regional dynamics, burgeoning right-wing movements with elite support, radical biosphere challenges like climate breakdown, and international military conflicts threatening terminal war.

Taken together, these factors figure into our everyday lives: the price of food and energy; costs of transportation; access to health care, childcare, and elder care; and housing and rental costs. And, in palpable ways, there are emotional costs as people feel insecure, as their communities are scapegoated, and as relatives at home and in faraway places are displaced and killed, by war and conflict.

If this dismal picture were a complete one, there would be little to be done and few meaningful choices to be made.

But this is not the case. In fact, for each concern, including the direst of existential threats, there are movements, organizations, and projects – as well as, yes, *politicians* – organizing for the things that we deserve. At the top level, we could speak, as this book does, about how workers, women, young people, elders, communities of color, peace and social justice activists, and many more are all addressing these issues and in many cases winning policies that matter even amid counter-movements.

DOI: 10.4324/9781003544371-2

And so it is that we can see a new assertive labor movement, winning contracts and wide public support, new members, and better conditions for all working people. In the constant struggle for gender equality and bodily autonomy, we see gains everywhere; each rollback met with a fightback. Even on climate change, the fossil fuel industry is losing the continuing battle for public opinion, creating openings for gains like those of the Inflation Reduction Act. In the struggle for racial and social justice, even in the face of the dubiously manufactured "wokeness" and "critical race theory" outrage, there is greater on-the-ground organizational sophistication, incredible youth-led organizing, and every "progressive issue" is now understood to require lenses of class, race, gender identity, and sexuality.

Even with the appointment of Justice Ketanji Brown Jackson, a historic progressive win that at the same time did not shift the power of the Supreme Court, there is a palpable sense of a "rising majority" whose values align closely with those of most progressives. Justice Jackson's elevation to the high court helped to reinvigorate calls for bold judicial reform, connected to a larger democracy movement.

However, even as we discern two clearly opposite trends, that of a right-wing authoritarian challenge against a still-congealing progressive majority at home, the global scene is a difficult one. The most dangerous of its elements are the ongoing and escalating wars in Ukraine and Palestine. These are followed closely by economic hostilities directed against a wide range of nation-states, with each threatening to erupt into armed confrontations.

Unlike the immediate post-Cold War era, however, the United States and its allies can no longer shape outcomes on their own. Instead, complex relationships with rising powers and changing global demographics demand a new era of peacemaking. But US peace movements and their global partners have not yet found the support they need in US foreign policy. Indeed, the opposite is true. The dominant forces shaping US foreign policy today, including the military-industrial complex, State Department, and corporate elites, seem incapable of expressing the peaceful ambitions of large majorities of the public. This disconnect is particularly evident in actions such as the attacks on Palestinians in Gaza and the alliances formed with the most extreme factions within Israeli society.

Quite apart from the assault on the inherent rights of the Palestinian people as recognized by the rest of humanity, US policy poses a huge dilemma for an evolving peace movement. Choosing between presidential candidates is not easy. Indeed, elements of the Republican Party can argue, with some justification, that their isolationism may make for a more peaceful world. Ironically, of course, such isolationism is exactly the opposite of what is needed in the face of an escalating climate breakdown. Not isolationism, but international cooperation of the sort that Noam Chomsky demands is not merely urgent but past due.

The choice in 2024 has uncanny similarities, however, to the 1968 elections. Then a relatively popular president, one who ushered in the "Great

Society" vision on the heels of a strong civil rights movement, found that his candidacy was no longer viable – largely a result of his unpopular wars abroad. To say that young people were not inspired is an understatement. Instead, they turned against him, producing not only protests at the Democratic National Convention in Chicago but also much abstentionism at the polls and even, in some cases, people voting for the right-wing candidate and Cold War warrior, Richard Nixon. That election, too, was consequential – a historic realignment of voting blocs occurred, laying the basis for the rise of Reagan Democrats and anti-black voting in the South.

Given these opposing forces at the national and global levels, how does this book help?

It is written for members of that overwhelming majority of US voters who, time and again, generation upon generation, respond to pollsters with strong support for progressive values. We will not rehearse them here. Instead, we have brought together informed opinions provided by on-the-ground activists, current elected officials, and engaged intellectuals. These opinions should provoke interesting conversations as well as useful talking points and organizing tips for engaging with both members of the public and closer-in people – relatives, neighbors, and coworkers.

In Part I, we address the big issues of the day, taking historical entry points around race, gender, and wealth inequality. We also look at specific issues as they relate to communities – housing, immigration, energy, workplace matters, and the like. However, we also specifically tease out the rise of right-wing authoritarianism in its manifold dimensions – its origins and current projects.

In Part II, we turn to organizing, including how we can engage with particular communities as voters, and how we talk with journalists and the media. Specifically undergirding this section is the question of turnout.

Between the two parts is an intermission, one that attends directly to the readers' most pressing questions. Anat Shenker-Osario speaks to our vision and messaging. In the "Letter to U.S. Students," three Boston College students give voice to the generational challenges of our time and the resulting feelings of outrage, but also of ambivalence with the choices offered. Notwithstanding their options, they end on a hopeful note. In doing so, they provide a set of concerns that no election strategist can afford to ignore. Young people must be won over. The intermission closes with the nuts and bolts of voting: how to register; how and where to cast your ballot; and how to get others to the polls so that they may also take advantage of the democratic space that is still available to them.

To continue this conversation in real time, the editors are maintaining an online platform: EmergencyElection.org. It hosts additional articles (see the Table of Contents) and curates new ones addressing this book's concern for democracy.

We allude to this democratic space because, as January 6, 2021, loudly proclaimed, we can no longer assume the peaceful transfer of office. In fact, more broadly speaking, such democratic spaces as social movements have won since the first elections in the United States – including ballot access, the right to vote, freedom of association, neutral courts, and peaceful debate – are all being challenged. As many people have pointed out, democracy itself is on the ballot. Our recognition of this threat, however, does not mean that the editors and contributors are mere partisans – our issues and concerns go beyond individual candidacies. Indeed, one progressive peace movement contributor to this book goes so far as to withhold her support from either of the two major parties' top-of-the-ticket candidates. Together with all other contributors, however, she recognizes the need for the active engagement of all voters. And it is to this end that we have assembled this book.

We believe that elections are consequential and that our agendas matter. The election of Andrew Jackson in 1828 had profound racial and class implications that we are still grappling with today. The compromise of 1877, which saw the election of Rutherford B. Hayes, ended Reconstruction and with it a foreclosing on the possibility of a racial and social democratic United States – for nearly 150 years. The election of Franklin Delano Roosevelt opened the door to a more democratic country, one friendlier to workers' rights, the rise of a middle class, and, for a brief time, global alliances against fascism. Of course, there are other similar examples of consequential elections.

In 2024, this book makes the case that we must hold onto our values and constituencies and vote strategically. Inevitably, this means making difficult choices up and down the ballot. In some cases, progressives will have to ask themselves to vote for candidates who may have positions they find repugnant and yet in whom their organizing may find a partner beyond election day.

In this sense, the options are fairly straightforward. Progressives have choices to make. They are active in social movements, they organize with workers in unions and into unions, and they revive rivers. They are rainbow-colored and respect distinct hues and histories even as they blend into other tones and movements. They recognize bodily autonomy even while understanding public goods and responsibilities so that life may be chosen and thrive, and, at a certain point, their colors turn a bright green before the fact of climate change. With all the implied values and priorities that ride on the backs of progressives, they are still tied to a straightforward question. Notwithstanding all our organizing, be it for the neighborhood garden, lead-free homes, or ceasefires abroad, *how do the elections of 2024 best serve our values and objectives?* The answer should be obvious – we must protect our democratic spaces, we must prosecute our agendas, we must organize our constituencies, and we must ensure the election of those with whom we can negotiate.

Part I

Voices and Visions, Communities and Key Issues

2 To Save Organized Human Society

Noam Chomsky

Editors: In 2020, Noam Chomsky opened Turnout! Mobilizing Voters in an Emergency *with a terse declaration about the role of activism. Not known for exaggerating, Chomsky declared that year to be a "fateful one" on which the future of humanity turns. We reprint that essay here, recognizing that each of Chomsky's points is all the more important and derives its urgency not only from the current electoral options but also from the critical social movement work that came before.*

It was not in doubt that 2020 would be a fateful year, especially for those who care enough about the world to try to determine its fate – for activists, in brief.

One reason is that 2020 brings us an election in the most powerful state in world history. Its outcome will have a major impact not only on the United States but, thanks to US power, on the perils faced by the entire world.

The nature and scale of these perils were underscored at the year's outset when the hands of the famous Doomsday Clock were set, providing as good a succinct assessment as we have of the state of the world. Since Donald Trump's election, the minute hand has been moved steadily toward midnight, meaning "it's over." As 2020 opened, the analysts abandoned minutes and turned to seconds: 100 seconds to midnight, the closest to terminal disaster since the first setting of the Clock in the wake of the atom-bomb attacks. The reasons were the usual ones: the severe and increasing threat of nuclear war and of environmental catastrophe, with the White House proudly in the lead in racing to the abyss; and the deterioration of functioning democracy, the one hope for dealing with impending disaster.

There is time to save organized human society (and many other species) from cataclysm, but not much. How much depends, in no small measure, on the US election in November 2020, which may turn out to be the most important election in human history, perhaps coming close to sealing the fate of organized human society.

Extreme words, but are they an exaggeration? Four more years of Trumpism might raise global warming to irreversible tipping points. At the very least, it would sharply raise the costs of assuring some measure of decent

DOI: 10.4324/9781003544371-4

survival. Trump's dismantling of the thin barriers to nuclear destruction might well succeed in setting off a final war; and even if not, it will drive the world closer to the brink. Another term will also provide Mitch McConnell with more time to pursue his assault on democracy by cramming the judiciary with enough young far-right justices to ensure that deeply reactionary and destructive policies will persist no matter what the public would prefer. For these reasons alone – there are many others – every effort must be expended to prevent this tragedy; and if it occurs, efforts must be redoubled to limit the damage and open the way to a livable world.

3 Mobilizing in Times of Emergency

Angela Lang

Editors: With this essay, we move to neighborhood, block-level voting and the experience of the converging crises of our time and as "full people" with complex and intersectional concerns.

It is no secret that the world has changed drastically over the last four years with the COVID pandemic. We are also in dire political times for our democracy. These things intersect when it comes to how we engage voters and how those voters show up at the polls. When conditions change, our tactics need to change as well. Nationally, we have seen a rise in hate crimes, violent political rhetoric, and continued attacks on voter rights. Locally in Milwaukee, we continue to be home to the most incarcerated zip code, which dramatically impacts how previously incarcerated people are able to participate in our democracy.

In Wisconsin, your voting rights are restored when you're "off paper" or off supervision. Many folks don't know that when they are off supervision, i.e., when their voting rights are restored. We encounter these same residents when we are knocking on doors. There was one time our Deputy Director, Keisha, spoke to a woman, and she said she couldn't vote because she was a felon. Many canvassers and outreach volunteers will say, "sorry, thank you for your time," and walk away. We train our teams to politely ask a follow-up, "Hey, I don't mean to be invasive, but do you mind me asking if you're off paper?" Keisha did just that, and it turns out this woman could have been voting for the last 15 years, and she didn't know she could. This is just one of the many stories that prove we need to do things differently to truly meet people where they are at.

What does it mean to meet people where they are at? A lot of us organizers say that, but there is no universal definition of how that looks. In Milwaukee, folks are hurting, and the policy wins that elected officials are touting aren't being felt by everyone. And folks *are* hurting—whether it is rebuilding your life after being released from prison or struggling to pay rent or childcare. Centering directly impacted people means understanding their full lives. Have you ever had a canvasser who was a no-call, no-show for their shift? I've seen organizations fire people and move on to the next person in line. In a world of

DOI: 10.4324/9781003544371-5

numbers-based measures, we sometimes lose sight of the issues we're fighting for. Our team of Ambassadors at Black Leaders Organizing for Communities (BLOC) are full people, and each and every one of us at BLOC is impacted by the same challenges we are fighting against. It serves as a reminder to know that people can be strong leaders and staff, and yet there isn't a full understanding of their personal lives. I remember we had a no-call, no-show for a team member, and when he showed up to the office a couple of days later, we asked him what happened. He said he had no money for the bus to get to work and his phone was cut off so he didn't have a way to communicate with us. We understood that real issues oftentimes trickle into your team, and they deserve just as much care and understanding as the same people we are trying to organize.

With these challenges, we have to organize differently. First and foremost, we can't continue to parachute into communities with no relationships and no context and tell them what they should be doing in their lives and in their communities. We need to have a "for us, by us" model and approach. While we love when folks outside our community want to get involved, it's important to have them plug in ways that make sense and don't make the community feel skeptical. As local organizers, we are the most trusted and strongest messengers, and we need to lean into that.

It's understandable that voters are feeling fatigued and exhausted with our political system. Promises are always made to earn our votes, but then there isn't always a strong delivery on those promises after we put them in office. With years and years of this vicious cycle, we need to understand and show compassion to the folks who feel that elections won't improve their living conditions. This is not the time to gaslight those voters and residents and shame them into voting for your candidate. In my experience, it further drives the voter away, and a lot of times comes across as condescending. We need to be bringing more people into our universe, not turning away those that are frustrated. There is a huge opportunity to do political education, dig into nuance, and have personal conversations to understand why people feel frustrated. When I was a union organizer, one of the things I learned was: Affirm, Answer, Redirect. It seems as if many of us have lost the "Affirm" part and go straight to Answer and Redirect without digging into the "why" of it all. In my opinion, it's a missed opportunity to not connect and relate to someone's struggle and see their humanity. More times than I can count, I've seen folks be shamed and talked down to after expressing their frustration. Not only is it offensive, it gaslights and shames voters. Would you be more willing to participate if someone responds to your frustrations in that way? I have knocked on doors myself where people said they are frustrated, and to that I respond, I agree. With the increase of wasted money on out-of-touch political consultants and glossy ads, the face-to-face conversation makes it personal and is an opportunity to break through the one-sided noise of mailers and TV ads.

Now, more than ever with multiple communities being attacked at once, it is important for us to build genuine, authentic coalition spaces that amplify everyone's voices and issues. Not all coalitions are built the same; some come to form naturally over a shared issue or goal. Other coalitions come together out of necessity because other coalitions or tables have not met their needs or have caused serious harm to their community. The most effective coalitions are the ones which are intersectional in their approach. A group fighting for a strong education system can be intersectional with how they talk about their work, given the deep relationships they have with organizations outside of their network and vice versa. Our issues rarely are single issues, and often when you peel back the layers, there are multiple systems of oppression at play in one issue. Having an intersectional lens brings people together, and many people can see "their" issues reflected in that "single" issue. When I first started organizing 17 years ago, one of the things we would ask ourselves was: "Is the issue widely and deeply felt?" By having an intersectional lens in our organizing, we expand the issue to more than the usual constituency base you organize. At this point in our political landscape, we need everyone to feel like they are a part of the kitchen-table issues and discussions.

We need everyone – right now. All hands on deck! There is an urgency in our issues, but that doesn't mean we need to rush humanity or rush our connections with each other. The core of organizing is relationships, not how many doors you can knock on or how many pledge cards you can get. In my opinion, those metrics don't tell the full story of the world we are trying to build. We need to be fierce in our tactics, urgent in our message, but intentional with building relationships over time. Power isn't something that is handed over easily, or simply won with an electoral outcome. This is a marathon, not a sprint, and it can be hard to reconcile that with today's urgent times. Voting isn't the silver bullet to all of our problems, but a tactic to build on as we seek liberation. Building something meaningful requires time and intentionality, but it can be difficult to do when it feels like everything is on fire around us. Nothing I'm saying is groundbreaking, and in between election cycles people agree, but when the final crunch comes, we sometimes sacrifice that intentionality and community building for a quick win that may not be sustainable. I challenge all of us to remember the core organizing values we learned and hold them close, no matter the circumstances.

4 How We Win for Women

Rachel O'Leary Carmona

Editors: Refusing to concede "an inch to rising authoritarianism," Carmona articulates a vision for a welcoming movement that takes a multipronged approach to empowerment, one that is plural, strategic, and ready for crises on the road to transformational change.

As we approach the 2024 elections, it becomes more and more clear that there is much at stake across the globe this year. With conflict and genocide raging in multiple countries, the public health and economic effects of COVID-19 still lingering, and the reemergence of a fascist former president threatening to have a massive impact on all branches of government, those of us who believe in justice have to seriously assess what it is we are facing and what we are willing to do about it.

This is especially true as it relates to women. A number of cases impacting access to reproductive care of all kinds are being heard in courts across the country this year. Additionally, right-wing legislators are working overtime to pass legislation that impedes upon women's right to control their own bodies. As the right continues to lose on abortion at the ballot box, they are doubling down on their efforts to undermine democracy at every turn.

There are no two ways about it: we *must* win in 2024. But to understand *how* we win in 2024 requires us to exercise rigor and discernment. There are a number of things we must examine: Who is the "we"? Why should we mobilize around voting? What is the crisis we face? What do we mean by win? I will attempt to answer these questions as they pertain to mobilizing the country's largest voter base, women.

How do we define our we? That subject has been a contentious one for the left for many years. With the rise of maximalism inside our movements,[1] it has been hard to arrive at shared strategies that get us to the scale we need to win. The Combahee River Collective statement teaches us that principled struggle demands that we understand that while oppression impacts different communities differently, each community has a role to play in the dismantling of these systems. The left must find ways to push past the in-group/out-group politics that keep our movement divided and shrinking.

DOI: 10.4324/9781003544371-6

We must reject the "othering" that has emerged from concepts like allyship or accomplicehood, or whatever the term du jour is, and recognize that everybody in the United States has to have skin in the game for the fight we have ahead. This is not to say that all the roles are the same or to undermine the necessity of specific and targeted organizations or strategies. Rather, it is an assertion that the idea that the movement is owned by a certain few, with everyone else needing to "check their privilege" rather than checking the ways in which we are all impacted and harmed by sexism, racism, and homophobia, has made our movement smaller than it needs to be to win.

We need to build our commitment to pluralism and organizing. It needs to become acceptable for people to come into the leftist movement without knowing everything or having complete agreement with the most current leftist litmus tests. Indeed, the very work of organizers is to meet our people where they are, assess their circumstances and needs, and build their political understanding and leadership. We must become comfortable with organizing alongside people whom we also hope to sharpen and move to the left. We move our base to our positions by building relationships and rigor, not by gatekeeping entrance to people who are partially aligned and, therefore, moveable. This is not an easy proposition. Because of our commitment to justice, to identity politics, and to plurality, our organizing mandate is more difficult than that of the opposition. But its difficulty makes it no less imperative.

Why voting? One thing the left continues to be in agreement on is the power of true democracy. While that may take many forms, we cannot continue to advocate for democracy around the world while diminishing the necessity of the electoral process in this country. Yes, there are many types of power we need to build beyond electoral, and there are many critiques we could and should levy – including the limitations of a two-party system, the dearth of viable candidate options that align with our politics, and what might be a principled stance when you disagree vehemently with the actions of the administration we are meant to support – but it is unwise to throw any political tactic away. When Malcolm X said, "By any means necessary," many of us took that to mean by ALL means.

Some groups are organizing protest votes. Some are organizing their people to boycott the election altogether, and not for the first time. I strongly disagree with the tactic of electoral boycott. Our politics must not be theoretical; they must exist within the context of our current conditions. The reality is that our mandate as organizers is to create as much ground under our feet as possible to fight for our people over time. This is not a facile argument about voting "Blue no matter who." This is a stance based on the unwillingness to cede an inch to fascists who would harm our communities.

It is a false claim to say there is no difference between the parties currently. One is pushing authoritarianism in open water. Refusing to vote in 2024 does not change conditions for anyone, except to make them more favorable for fascists. This situation is yet another one that demands rigor from us.

Withholding a vote from Democrats to punish the Biden administration would usher in the conditions for our community to be at greater harm and immediate risk. We must be strategic at this moment, recognizing that, just as in the Civil Rights Movement, voting is not the vision, nor is it the strategy; it is simply one among a host of tactics to move us closer to the world we envision.

What is the crisis we face? The crisis we face is multifaceted. Globally, authoritarian forces are on the rise, each seeking to roll back hard-won rights. Domestically, we battle pressures from neo-liberals to moderate our agendas, as well as impractical radical pressure that prioritizes ideological purity over tangible progress.

To overcome these challenges, we need a multi-pronged approach that fosters thought leadership, embraces diverse tactics, and builds power from the grassroots up – not just top-down party dictates. Winning the election is crucial but insufficient; we must organize at a scale that sustains our victories through enduring governance.

In 2020 and 2022, we fell short of defending hard-won gains. But by rejecting false unity and brand building, and by cultivating a movement that values pluralism, strategic voting, crisis readiness, and grassroots empowerment, we can forge a path to transformative change that uplifts all women and members of society.

The way forward will not be easy, but our collective power is immense when we unite behind a common vision of justice and equity. It can be done. Together, we can energize voters, shape bold agendas, and create the future we need – a future where all women thrive. By 2050, we can be a feminist-led movement that ensures anyone and everyone has the freedom to lead empowered lives in safety and security in their bodies, in their communities, and throughout the country.

Note

1 Maurice Mitchell, "Building Resilient Organizations: Toward Joy and Durable Power in a Time of Crisis," *Convergence*, November 29, 2022, https://convergencemag.com/articles/building-resilient-organizations-toward-joy-and-durable-power-in-a-time-of-crisis/.

5 The Fascist Threat and the Progressive Agenda

Charles Derber

Editors: Reviewing the troubling parallels between the rise of Hitler and the MAGA project, Derber cautions against progressive complacency. Instead, he urges the building of "a bold new progressive coalition for deep economic and social change."

The 2024 election has not only intensified fears about an American breed of fascism but has turned attention specifically to the rise of Hitler in Germany. This is not only because Trump began using Hitler's famous phrases about crushing the "vermin" who are "poisoning our blood." The rise of Hitler has broader, alarming parallels to the rise of Trump, though there are also important differences. We need to learn vital lessons to prevent any similar US disaster in 2024 and beyond.

Hitler gained power, much as Trump has, by choosing to engage in the political arena and building a base among conservative parties and rural, non-college farmers, workers, and small business people. While Hitler started as an insurrectionist, his infamous 1923 "beer hall" putsch in Bavaria failed, and he was thrown in jail, where he wrote his Nazi manifesto, *Mein Kampf.* Released after eight months, Hitler shifted his strategy, building political power in the electoral arena, while simultaneously using militias and violence to threaten and kill opponents. This is the first great parallel to Trump: engaging in mainstream political parties and elections while using unconstitutional threats and violence to unravel the very electoral politics he was using to gain power.

Hitler appealed to a wide base of rural and working-class Germans who hated the German establishment because of the humiliating terms of surrender after World War I, which led to hyper-inflation and extreme economic precariousness. Hitler blamed urban liberal aliens and globalist cosmopolitan elites, especially Jews. He promised to make Germany great again by personally delivering jobs and pride to German Aryans. Ironically, he delivered many of his promises through massive spending on the military, the *autobahn,* and social services for Aryans. In the US, Trump also promised relief to working people suffering from inflation and insecure jobs created by the current cosmopolitan globalist establishment, promising that he would invest in America to rebuild the nation's economy and pride, while destroying "enemies of the people."

DOI: 10.4324/9781003544371-7

Hitler was crystal clear about his plans. In his speeches and writings, he spelled out how he would lead a political movement to overthrow the immoral urban Marxists and cultural elites with college education who betrayed Aryan Germans. While he constantly ranted about his anti-democratic plans, his wild language and political actions were normalized by much of the German public and the German conservative establishment. Some Germans simply dismissed him as a charismatic blowhard, while many farmers and workers who did believe his violent outbursts liked his anger and voted for him. They thought he would rebuild Germany with his nationalist agenda, personally delivering the goods that the cosmopolitan globalist "democracy" had taken away.

The parallels with Trump are striking. Trump maintains his political legitimacy among millions of Americans who have gotten accustomed to his violent rhetoric and either ignore it or like it. Some dismiss the liberal media attack on Trump as partisan exaggeration; they don't take seriously the warnings about fascism and the "death of democracy" on MSNBC and CNN. Many others – white ordinary American farmers, workers, and small businesspeople – believe and love Trump's rhetoric. They feel the current liberal "democratic system" brings them nothing and that Trump will personally fix it all.

Another parallel: Hitler was a master of cultural messaging, using Nazi films, visual symbols, art, music, and religion to great effect. Culture personalizes politics, and excites and inspires voters. Trump is also a cultural showman, who viscerally moves millions with tweets, culture wars, racism, and religion; meanwhile, progressives lose voters with their own siloed version of cultural identity politics while winning others with film stars like Robert De Niro or Matt Damon and celebrity singers like Taylor Swift.

Another historical parallel: German corporations thought they could control Hitler and prevent him from carrying out the horrors he promised in his speeches and writing. The same became true of Trump, who was seen by big donor corporations as somebody they could ultimately control. At the summer 2023 Davos annual meeting of global corporate elites, there was concern about Trump. But the majority of the uber-wealthy concluded that Trump would be no serious threat to corporate interests – and that they could stop his worst violence or coups. Many also felt the system was getting too "woke" and leftist, and they continued to fund the MAGA GOP.

As Hitler built his political power, German liberals and leftists attacked each other, often ignoring Hitler and failing to build the coalition that could mobilize millions of anti-fascist Germans and link anti-fascist political parties. They desperately needed to join forces to prevent Hitler from becoming the Fuehrer while offering a progressive agenda to save Germany from its crises. Their failure on both counts ensured Hitler's fascist takeover of Germany.

This is a key lesson for progressives today. First, they need to take MAGA seriously both as a neo-fascist movement and a political party that can win elections and quickly install authoritarian rule. As I have shown with Yale Magrass in a 2024 book, *Who Owns Democracy?*,[1] there is a long tradition of

American fascism, a violent politics based on racial caste power and intersecting with corporate power, starting in the slave South and sustained through the fascist ghosts of Jim Crow after the Civil War. The MAGA movement speaks to deeply rooted Southern white Christian and nationalist sensibilities.

The German experience also makes clear that a civil society with historical strains of authoritarianism can quickly turn to dictatorship or neo-fascist rule. It took about three months for Hitler to assume total control after becoming the highest vote-getter and being put in power by conservative political leaders in January 1933. Hitler soon delivered the violent retribution that many Germans had ignored or disbelieved. As the fascist crisis became more real, many Germans felt Hitler was doing the right thing by remilitarizing the nation, creating jobs, and eliminating the vermin.

Trump in victory will try to do something similar, implementing Project 2025, his explicit manifesto for eliminating the independent judiciary and civil service, building massive deportation camps, gutting civil rights and personal freedoms, and putting the entire political system under his personal control.[2] Like Germans who followed Hitler, many ordinary working Americans will be happy to join a long-term MAGA attack on a "democracy" which has abandoned them.

It is true that as Hitler rose to power, the German economy was in a deep depression, far worse than the US economy in 2024. But US workers rated Biden's economy as poor and preferred Trump to Biden on the economy. This reflects the reality that about half of American working-class people say they live precariously, paycheck to paycheck, unable to pay soaring rents or grocery bills, fearing that one job loss or illness will sink them into poverty.

Because of all the online threats incited by Trump in his 2024 campaign, Democrats running for federal office and ordinary election workers had to get armed security protection for themselves and their families. But most Americans did not pay attention, and many rural folks and non-college workers welcomed the rising violent threats that could further erode a democracy that labels them "deplorable."

Anti-fascists have to rally together in a vast coalition in 2024 and beyond to prevent an American fascist revival and takeover. This pro-democracy coalition must unite diverse political communities – independents, moderates, liberals, and Leftists – with bold promises to shake up the ruling system better than MAGA, both to prevent fascism and deliver the goods to a population that "democracy" has abandoned. They can only win with a progressive agenda solving people's problems and exciting their vote, requiring major public investments and "power to the workers/power to the people" in health care, infrastructure, and in US corporations – along with cultural "Swifties."

This agenda also requires an emergency program to stop climate change to excite the progressive base while creating millions of new good jobs for workers worried about losing their jobs in coal mining, fracking gas or drilling oil. It also has to be combined with an outspoken commitment to end Biden's wars, essential for turning out the base and investing in American jobs.

Defeating American fascism now means taking on much of the system that Trump and MAGA also attack, but with progressive boldness and real long-term change for the people; building a movement against MAGA also means building a strong progressive movement against the policies of centrist Democrats well beyond the 2024 election. This doesn't mean abandoning centrist candidates in the election who are not progressive enough and have promoted terrible wars, but remain anti-fascist. Many progressive Germans didn't want to support the tepid parties of the center and left that had Parliamentary power. Here is the stark truth ringing through the history of fascist electoral threats: you must vote for a candidate you don't like if failing to do so brings fascist disaster. But you can and should support such an anti-fascist candidate only as you forcefully oppose many of his domestic and foreign policies and fight aggressively to change them. Your vote is an emergency move to prevent fascism but also a way to buy time and build the progressive policies that excite you.

In a close emergency election, your vote matters. And your vote carries moral value and suasion because it *is* the beginning of a renewed movement for the progressive ideals that your candidate or party will have to respond to as you fight long-term with a revived and bold new progressive coalition for deep economic and social change that is the only way to prevent fascism.

Notes

1 Charles Derber and Yale R. Magrass, *Who Owns Democracy: The Real Deep State and the Struggle Over Class and Caste in America* (New York and London: Routledge, 2024), https://www.routledge.com/Who-Owns-Democracy-The-Real -Deep-State-and-the-Struggle-Over-Class-and-Caste-in-America/Derber-Magrass /p/book/9781032781907.
2 "Project 2025 | Presidential Transition Project," accessed April 30, 2024, https:// www.project2025.org/.

6 Political Violence – Old and New, Neither Acceptable

Suren Moodliar

As Anthony King lay dying in his yard, his wife tearfully reported to a 911 operator that he had been shot – three bullets to his head – by Mr. Austin Coombs, a neighbor in their small Ohio town. Mrs. King explained to the operator, Coombs has "come over, like, four times confronting my husband because [Coombs] thought [that her husband] was a Democrat." Indeed Mr. King was actually a conservative white Republican but died a suspected Democrat. The Kings' tragic story opens a 2023 special report on political violence by the Reuters news agency.[1] The story of the 10 African American shoppers killed by a white supremacist at their grocery store in Buffalo, NY, in May 2022, concludes a painful list of anecdotes shared in the report's introduction.

Reuters' widely cited and oft-quoted study has a simple thesis: political violence is on the rise in the United States, with nearly a fifth of the electorate finding violence acceptable in the furtherance of political objectives. It is also presented as something characteristic of both right- and left-wing "extremes." Their introduction also reflects a studied style of American political commentary: violence visited on white people, e.g., the Kings, merits individual attention and concern, while that inflicted on black people can be retold via a simple statistic, 10 dead in Buffalo.

For progressives, intent on preserving and expanding such democratic openings as have been wrought from our old constitutional order, violence is a particularly challenging topic. We want to recognize both the deep history of violence in this settled continent *and* the new turns accompanying rising neofascism. At the same time, we also need to make careful distinctions about what counts as violence in a "post-truth" era. How, after all, are we to distinguish between mere rule-breaking and destruction of property, which often accompanies civil disobedience and mass movements, from oppressive violence, necessarily part of the neofascist project, aimed at thwarting the democratic will or denying civil rights?

Fortunately, these are answerable questions. First, we must recognize the intellectual operations that mystify the analysis of political violence, and then we must understand and celebrate the lessons from the history of

DOI: 10.4324/9781003544371-8

challenging state, racist, and fascist violence. At the outset, however, as we will show below, we need to recognize the relative novelty of direct, overt support for political violence from the political leadership of the Republican Party and its standard bearer, former president Donald J. Trump. Right-wing and often centrist discourse engage in three intellectual maneuvers that prevent fruitful conversations about violence. First, activities or incidents are *decontextualized* and redefined, next they are relativized through *false equivalences*, and finally, the blame is *deflected* onto a real or often conjured scapegoat.

Decontextualization: In the spring of 2024, while global public opinion was rankled by the ongoing genocide in Gaza, progressives watched in horror as Republican demagogues hauled university presidents before Congress. The pathetic responses of the academic leaders – at best equivocating or, worse, capitulating on complex questions of political rhetoric and academia – exemplify the "decontextualization" operation.

Channeling Senator Joseph McCarthy of the 1950s, Representative Elise Stefanik,[2] then a prospective Trump running mate, reduced normal campus debate about global issues to a simplified matter of hate speech and, by extension, implied violence. As with McCarthy-era tragedies, the college presidents had an opportunity to rise to the occasion and reject Stefanik's framing out of hand, much as people like Paul Robeson had done during the Cold War.[3] Instead, we were treated to painful congressional spectacles in which college presidents were unable to effectively answer bullying politicians.

Stefanik defined the debate: "Does calling for the genocide of Jews violate Harvard's rules on bullying and harassment?" she demanded of a flummoxed Claudine Gay, then President of Harvard University. "It can be, depending on the context," the hapless Gay averred. Moving in for the kill, Stefanik cut off Gay and suggested that campus rhetoric about Israeli violence was equivalent to "committing genocide." Stefanik's browbeating of the presidents proceeded smoothly: campus rhetoric and debate were shorn of the underlying acts – the ongoing massacre of more than 30,000 Palestinians – and equated with Hamas' military actions, which, in turn, the media suggested, were a continuation of the Nazi genocide.

The complexity of the campus, the academic freedom to explore the history of occupation and resistance, the diversity of student responses to faraway events involving threatened and dying family and friends, real policy debates over failed "peace processes" or even global and regional rivalries were all rendered invisible by Stefanik's simple question.[4] Unlike Robeson, who was accountable to a struggle and people's movement, the flustered campus presidents were no match for the rapacious Stefanik. In a few hearings, the MAGA congressperson redefined the national debate over the Middle East. This set the stage for a violent spring in which anti-violence, pro-Palestine student encampments were set up for violent repression from both counter-protestors and the police.

False equivalences: The inability to either defend free speech or condemn structural violence in plain English left the college presidents appearing foolish. More consequentially, it surrendered the liberal mainstream conversation to right-wing abstractions about the "violence of the left" and alleged "antisemites."

Ironically, Stefanik's politics and those of her movement condone real acts of violence by the MAGA base and leader. On January 6, 2021, at the urging of their national leader, Donald J. Trump, the MAGA base attacked Congress in a failed attempt to disrupt the constitutionally mandated transfer of executive power to the legitimate winner of the 2020 US presidential election.[5] It resulted in several deaths and injuries to hundreds of individuals, including 174 police personnel.[6] Initial responses from Republican elites reflected the normal confusion associated with any breaking, disruptive event. However, one early theme, quickly dispelled but never fully eliminated, was the idea that the January 6 insurrection could be laid at the feet of "antifa."[7] Ridiculous on its face, the attempt was not merely to deflect responsibility from the real authors but was also an attempt to build on an elite construct, antifa as a modern, coordinated, national, if not global, formation aimed at destroying US society. However, as Randy Blazak of the Oregon Coalition Against Hate Crime notes, "They [the Right] used antifa as sort of a kind of simplification of the forces they face on the left. And it serves them well because it rallies people."

Building on the political construction of the "antifa," however poorly grounded it may be in the real world, is necessary for the "both side-ism" trope of centrist politics, mainstream media, and Hollywood. Indeed, witness the ultimate expression of this trope, the 2024 blockbuster movie, "Civil War." It allows director Alex Garland to describe himself as "apolitical."[8] The movie turns on an ingenious device of ambivalence – "the antifa massacre." Was it a massacre *of* or *by* antifa? Equivalence through ambivalence.

The device and its uncertainty, however, are belied by a profound asymmetry: the modern source of violence is not one in which right and left are equally implicated. By and large, political violence finds its roots in right-wing activity driven both by the US's foundation myths as well as encouragement from above. Consider, for example, the paradigmatic case of the 2020 unrest in Portland, Oregon. Mainstream media suggested that the state was essentially riven between warring MAGA and antifa factions. This suggestion is no mere historical coincidence. It was one promoted by then-President Trump. After raging against an imagined antifa for years, in June 2020, in response to the George Floyd mobilizations, Trump deployed federal police "to protect" national monuments and sites against antifa and "anarchists and assorted radicals." Upending conservative lore about "states' rights," this deployment took place regardless of the objections from states' governors and cities' mayors.

Democratic Party-leaning Oregon, however, produced the single national instance of someone who characterized himself as "antifa" and who acknowledged that he killed a member of the Patriot Prayer, a far-right, pro-Trump faction. In this case, however, circumstances around both the initial killing of the far-rightist and the subsequent quasi-execution of the antifa follower are shrouded in uncertainties: was the initial act one of self-defense? Was the antifa follower merely executed, contrary to federal claims? Whatever the answers to these questions, what is certain is that the primary source of political violence involving people (as opposed to property) comes from the right. In the Reuters study of recent political violence that they studied and that resulted in 39 deaths, the perpetrators came overwhelmingly from the right. Where they implicate the left in recent violence, it is in regard to the destruction of property – usually ranging from graffiti to window breaking, i.e., acts of vandalism.

Right-wing violence is aimed at people; the altogether more minor actions on the left point to rule-breaking deliberately *not directed at people.* According to Michael Loadenthal, who has studied more than 21,000 violent incidents from ecological activism between 1973 and 2010, 99.9% caused "zero injury." Where four fatalities occurred, these involved individuals unconnected to the left.[9] The much more recent Reuters study notes that of the 14 fatalities since the January 6 Insurrection (and August 2023), 13 perpetrators had clear right-wing affiliations and only one had left connections.Ned Parker and Peter Eisler, Political Violence in Polarized U.S. at Its Worst since 1970s, , August 9, 2023, https://www.reuters.com/investigates/special-report /usa-politics-violence/.[10]

No doubt there are many reasons for this asymmetry, but what is plainly visible (and audible) is that right-wing anger and violence are consistently and carefully nurtured by right-wing elites using false narratives of victimhood. Victim-in-Chief, of course, is Donald Trump, who routinely rails against the left, "antifa," communists, and, more rarely, "fascist" persecution. More overtly, in the above-noted Oregon tragedy, he exhorted federal officers "to get him," by which many rightly understood he meant to kill the antifa activist, someone who was known to be seeking a peaceful resolution.[11] Violent rhetoric from Trump has only increased, reaching its current fever pitch in the context of his many criminal indictments and civil case losses. So, when Reuters complains about a new wave of violence, it should not engage in false equivalences and two-side-ism. Political violence on the right exists because it is legitimated at the highest levels of the Republican elite.

One further problem with the Reuters study is that it declined to include police killings and other actions as evidence of political violence. The ruthless suppression of student encampments by the Texas National Guard, the Los Angeles Police Department, and the New York Police Department, to name only a few high-profile recent cases, escapes Reuters' purview. While it is not within the scope of this essay to consider the obvious problems with their selective vision, it does point to the long-standing problem of *official* violence predating the American republic itself. In the earliest colonies, acting in the name of the British crown, settlers imported total war-making strategies and tactics from Europe's Eighty Years War.[12] The extreme violence and attempts to annihilate "the enemy" shocked indigenous people whose own warmaking was altogether more restrained. This heritage, which elaborated itself over several centuries of policing aimed at enforcing an unjust racial and class order, may help explain the restricted lenses of centrist politics and the mainstream media. More pertinently, it also provides the rationale for current right-wing violence, which sees itself as achieving political ends the way "our forefathers" did.

Given this inheritance and current neofascist rhetoric and organizing, how are progressives to respond? If our history is a guide, we must reject false binaries of electoral and movement politics and organize on all fronts – voting strategically in elections and building broad movements. If the right and some centrists have chosen to demonize "antifa," this mystification must be challenged.

Deflection: As noted earlier, antifa and other real and imagined actors have been scapegoated and blamed for violence – this includes the astounding Trumpist claims about immigrants and about transgender communities.[13] To be clear, the vilification of immigrants and other communities is not confined to Trump, but includes state-level legislative attempts at excluding, for example, transgender and non-binary people from elected office, public restrooms, or even updating their driving licenses.[14] By casting these communities as responsible for "America's decline," such legislation effectively legitimates violence against them and anyone who advocates for them.

If the tenor of this essay is to associate recent political violence with the right and with an oppressive state, we must also be conscious of the fact that a majority of US residents reject violence. While this fact is reassuring, it will require an organized and united front drawn from this majority to thwart an oppressive and minoritarian regime of violence from coming to power. The left has a rich history of coalition building against fascism, sometimes successful as in the global effort to defeat Hitler and Mussolini, sometimes less so as exemplified by the rise of those actors in the first place. That said, a turn to politics and organizing on the part of the left, particularly as it organizes across a wide range of concerns that have majoritarian potential – from mitigating climate change to increasing working-class power to rejecting warmaking in the Middle East and Ukraine – as well as making connects with long-standing resistance traditions in the United States, is the only promising avenue to fight violence. If there is hope, one of the places from which it comes is from the victims of violence themselves. Mark Talley, son of Geraldine C. Talley who was gunned down in Buffalo, has gone on to organize against violence, setting up an organization and campaign; he explains,

I am yet to tell you that no one deserves to experience this kind of tragedy, and that we must do something to end this cycle of violence. We can't allow these weapons to be used in such a way, and we must take concrete steps to make sure this never happens again. America is suffering from a malady that manifests itself in racism, homophobia, xenophobia, an unhealthy fixation on guns, a refusal to acknowledge the most dangerous thing in the world is a young adult White male, and most significantly, socioeconomic inequality. Sadly America appears to be either too scared or too unwilling to seek medical attention for its affliction.[15]

And yet, Talley persists.

Notes

1 Ned Parker and Peter Eisler, "Political Violence in Polarized U.S. at Its Worst since 1970s," *Reuters*, August 9, 2023, https://www.reuters.com/investigates/special-report/usa-politics-violence/.
   At the time of writing, the latest available report on the consequences of the November 22 shooting is that Austin Combs has not yet been deemed competent to stand trial. See Lauren Pack, "New Evaluations for Local Man Accused of Killing Neighbor Because of Politics," *[Butler County] Journal-News*, March 18, 2024, https://www.journal-news.com/crime/new-evaluations-for-local-man-accused-of-killing-neighbor-because-of-politics/EIHUUWRRQ5FJXHFGX5OLS2GWGU/.
2 Nicholas Fandos, "Elise Stefanik Has Gained Widespread Attention in Antisemitism Hearings," *The New York Times*, May 23, 2024, sec. U.S., https://www.nytimes.com/2024/05/23/us/elise-stefanik-republican-antisemitism-hearings.html.
3 "June 12, 1956: Paul Robeson Testifies Before HUAC," *Zinn Education Project*, accessed June 1, 2024, https://www.zinnedproject.org/news/tdih/paul-robeson-testifies-before-huac/.
4 Richard Pape's allegedly "non-partisan" study of student attitudes suggests that both Jewish and Muslim students experience fear and a sense of persecution on US campuses. However, this approach is based on student perceptions and blurs the lines between perceptions and actual acts of violence. See Richard Pape, *Understanding Campus Fears After October 7 and How to Reduce Them* (Chicago: University of Chicago, Chicago Project on Security and Threats, March 7, 2024), https://d3qi0qp55mx5f5.cloudfront.net/cpost/i/docs/CPOST_Understanding_Campus_Fears_-_Report.pdf?mtime=1709832445.
5 While most accounts are highly contested, interested readers may explore the detailed "Final Report of the Select Committee to Investigate the January 6th Attack on the United States Capitol," *GovInfo.gov*, December 22, 2024, https://www.govinfo.gov/content/pkg/GPO-J6-REPORT/html-submitted/index.html.
   A survey by the Chicago Project on Security and Threats found that 5% of Americans believed force was justified to restore Trump to the presidency. Today, that number is the same, at 5%. In our new survey, we also asked those who neither agreed nor disagreed about their leaning and found 12% of these, or four million, lean toward agreeing that force is justified to restore Trump. This suggests our previous surveys have underestimated the true level of support for Trump by effectively counting all the ambivalent as not agreeing. When we add these four million from the ambivalent to the explicit support for force to restore Trump, we now have a more accurate estimate of the size of the insurrectionist movement – as of

April 2023, about 17 million. (See CPOST's new, "Political and Violent Dangers to Democracy Tracker," https://cpost.uchicago.edu/publications/april_2023_survey _report_introducing_cposts_new_political_and_violent_dangers_to_democracy _tracker/)

6 Even these numbers should be treated as complex, freighted as they are by definitions and time frames. See Chris Cameron, "These Are the People Who Died in Connection With the Capitol Riot," *The New York Times*, January 5, 2022, sec. U.S., https://www.nytimes.com/2022/01/05/us/politics/jan-6-capitol-deaths.html.

7 Meg Anderson, "antifa Didn't Storm the Capitol. Just Ask the Rioters," *NPR*, March 2, 2021, sec. Investigations, https://www.npr.org/2021/03/02/972564176/ antifa-didnt-storm-the-capitol-just-ask-the-rioters.

8 Matt Zoller Seitz, "Civil War Movie Review and Film Summary," *RogerEbert .com*, accessed June 1, 2024, https://www.rogerebert.com/reviews/civil-war-movie -review-2024.

9 Loadenthal as cited in Andreas Malm, *How to Blow up a Pipeline: Learning to Fight in a World on Fire, Electronic Book, EPUB version* (London & New York: Verso, 2021), p. 89.

10 Ned Parker and Peter Eisler, "Political Violence in Polarized U.S. at Its Worst since 1970s," Reuters, August 9, 2023, https://www.reuters.com/investigates/special-report/usa-politics-violence/

11 For more context, see Jonathan Levinson, "Newly Un-Redacted Report Shows How Feds Politicized Response to 2020 Portland Protests," Oregon Public Broadcasting, October 27, 2024, https://www.opb.org/article/2022/10/27/newly-un-redacted-report-shows-how-feds-politicized-response-to-2020-portland-protests/.

12 See John Grenier, *The First Way of War: American War Making on the Frontier, 1607–1814* (Cambridge: Cambridge University Press, 2008).

13 Nathan J. Robinson, "Take Trump Seriously When He Vows To Build The Camps," *Current Affairs*, November 13, 2023, https://www.currentaffairs.org/2023/11/take -trump-seriously-when-he-vows-to-build-the-camps.

Mariel E. Addis, "Terrified about What Trump Win Would Mean," *Daily Hampshire Gazette*, February 8, 2024, https://www.gazettenet.com/Guest-column-ist-Addis-53936258.

14 Orion Rummler, "More States Are Pushing to Stop Legally Recognizing Trans People in Public Life," *The 19th*, January 24, 2024, https://19thnews.org/2024/01/ transgender-state-bills-legal-recognition/.

This is not a one-way fight, one without resistance. See, for examples: Quinn Yeargain, "Challenging Anti-Trans Legislation Under State Constitutions," *State Court Report*, July 11, 2023, https://statecourtreport.org/our-work/analysis-opinion /challenging-anti-trans-legislation-under-state-constitutions; "LGBTQ+ Advocacy & Government Affairs & Government Affairs – The Trevor Project," accessed June 1, 2024, https://www.thetrevorproject.org/advocacy/.

15 Mark Talley, *5/14: The Day the Devil Came to Buffalo* (Kindle Direct Publishing, 2022), p. 137.

7 The Dystopian Vision of Project 2025

Joe Guinan

Editors: As you know, many on the far right have been learning the lessons of the Trump administration, 2017–2020, and are preparing to do things better. "Better," at least, from their point of view. Can you tell us about Project 2025, which is quite overt about their extreme agenda?

Joe Guinan: Frankly, I am concerned that they're more organized than we are. The thing to say about Project 2025 is that it's important to study because it helps get us beyond that cartoon view of who our opponents are. It's a very daunting counterpoint to our own efforts because if you look at it, it's incredibly well-resourced and organized.

They've got 100 of the leading organizations on the right, led by the Heritage Foundation, aiming to ensure that the next conservative administration, a Trump administration, a *second* Trump administration, would be far more successful in their terms than the first because they would be prepared at the level of personnel. They would be getting more hard-nosed and hard-right people who won't abandon Trump at the first sign of difficulty.

They've also had a program transforming the entire federal government agency by agency. It would be a 180-day blitz of the apparatus of the state. They are pushing a politics focusing on the pain points in the present crisis in their own terms. We see the Cold War against China replacing the prior commitments to globalization and free trade. We see their recognition of the fact that they haven't been able to shrink the size of the public sector as a share of GDP. They are going to take another run at doing that – reducing the size of the state – through an assault on the administrative state, the downsizing or abolition of certain departments, and replacing civil servants with political ideologues committed to dismantling, overhauling, or repurposing the machinery of government.

Their track record suggests this is the best approximation that we've got for what they're going to do! The Heritage Foundation is quite open. The first time they did something like this was for Reagan, and I think about 30% of their proposals to the Reagan administration were taken up by that administration. They boast that for the first Trump administration, that rose to something

DOI: 10.4324/9781003544371-9

like 66% of their recommendations, and their goal for Project 2025 is that 80% of what they propose becomes policy.

There are questions we could ask about the likelihood of their success given the broad sweep of what we've seen through Republican and Democratic presidents alike since the 1970s. Reagan himself failed on many of their indicators. But the concern is not that they're suddenly going to be able to pull this off whereas they haven't before. The problem is the disruption and pain that would be caused in the process of what they're doing and how much collateral damage and continued deterioration and decay would result. And certainly, from their point of view, it's a wise strategy to dismantle some of the programs and agencies progressives seek to build as we move from a Green New Deal to a green, democratically planned, and overhauled economy.

We should study Project 2025 because it gives us a real sense of where they've shifted and where politics has forced them to go. They see the hostility to big tech and the big platforms, the popular turn away from free trade. They are not all on the same page; there's a debate about free trade versus fair trade within Project 2025, indicative of the de-globalizing move of politics in response to the globalization crisis. But they are a whole lot better resourced and organized and on the same page than progressives are – and ready to go from day one. Literally from, "So help me God," as the starting gun to a blitz that would probably see some major efforts, like trying to deport a million people in the first month and things like that.

We should be studying them so that we're ready for what they're going to try, and also because, frankly, it shows a level of seriousness and engagement with the scale and scope of our national and global challenges that we on the -left haven't really begun to grapple with ourselves.

Editors: We hear you ringing the alarm bells. Who else is ringing the alarm bells? And are we sufficiently networked? Are we aspiring to be better networked?

Joe: I'm kind of shocked at how little attention there's been to Project 2025, which became a book that has sold out. You can't get a hard copy. But it's been out there now for well over a year and has been circulating. It's happening in plain sight. The web portal's up there for people to sign up so their names can be considered for positions in the administration, etc. And yet very few people discuss it. I only noticed this a couple of months ago for the first time because it was brought to my attention.

The place where I'm seeing the most attention to this really is unsurprisingly among communities of color. Some of the radical political leadership is really paying attention to this effort, as one person described it to me, not just to take us back to the 1950s, but to the 1850s in terms of racial politics. And so, I think certain sections of our base are hearing this loud and clear because of the real and present danger and material threat that it clearly poses to their well-being and safety. But there's a whole bunch of us, certainly on the economic justice side of things and in more mainstream base-building circles, that aren't, at least publicly, talking about this.

We should direct people to it to show the threat in its full shape and form. Not that everything is in there, but it at least shows the order of magnitude of what they're going to try and do. It's spelled out in their own words, so we ought to be direct in response. Half of the hits on their website should be from us, people who are looking at what's going on there, alerting themselves to the danger, and then using it to educate people through our networks.

This is not about Joe Biden and Gaza. This is about the scope and scale of the federal government and of government in general. It is about the safety net, the balance between capital and labor, and many other things that are really on the table in this election.

8   Billionaires vs. Your Vote

Chuck Collins

There are two things that are important in politics. The first is money, and I can't remember what the second one is.– Ohio Senator Mark Hanna, 1895

If you don't vote, the billionaires win.

The wealthiest people in the USA are happy to see you turn away in cynicism and disgust. They would be pleased if you stayed home on Election Day or threw away your vote on a symbolic losing candidate. Your inaction will make the billionaires – and their political enablers – very, happy.

But here's the dirty little secret they don't want you to know: the rich don't always win. And when it comes to elections, the ultra-wealthy don't always get what they want. Your vote, in certain circumstances, can matter.

The wealthiest people in this country – and the corporations they control – are used to getting their way. Over the last four decades, wealth inequality has grown to extreme levels. The wealthy and powerful have rigged the rules of the economy to get more wealth and power. As a result, the lion's share of the income and wealth gains have flowed to the top one percent – with most flowing to the top one-tenth of one percent, folks with over $30 million.[1]

The billionaire class has lobbied successfully to shift taxes off themselves and onto you, to keep wages low, and regulation toothless. On March 18, 2020, a week into the 2020 COVID-19 pandemic, there were 615 billionaires in the US with a total combined wealth of $2.9 trillion. Four years later, on March 18, 2024, there were 737 billionaires with a total combined wealth of $5.5 trillion, a four-year gain of 88 percent.[2] These wealth gains are a testament to the power of the wealthiest few to extract financial rewards, even during a period of tremendous adversity and loss.

This wealthiest 0.1 percent are very politically engaged and are BUY-Partisan – willing to finance and influence politicians in any political party. They celebrate political gridlock and dysfunction, as inaction keeps the non-wealthy from putting forward policies premised on the ideal that the economy should work for everyone, not just the ultra-wealthy.

One of the few risks to oligarchic rule is democratic elections when the people's agenda might thwart the wishes and interests of the ultra-wealthy.

DOI: 10.4324/9781003544371-10

For this reason, the billionaire class is highly engaged in politics, investing in candidates, lobbying, and influencing regulations and rules.

The Wealth Primary. One of the first ways that billionaires disenfranchise everyone else is through what Rep. Jamie Raskin calls "the wealth primary." Long before a candidate for office stands before voters on primary or election day, wealthy donors have winnowed and weaned the field, voting with their dollars as to who stands for election. Candidates with views dissenting from the donor class rarely appear on the ballot.

Large campaign contributions, which only a small sliver of the US public are able to make, mold and shape the field. Woe be to a candidate who is neither independently wealthy nor surrounded by wealthy supporters. Thanks to partisan gerrymandering of political districts, the primary is often the decisive day, not the final election. As a result, a tiny sliver of donors and engaged voters generally determine the outcome of races long before Election Day.

Campaign Finance. Campaign cash is the critical and often decisive factor in determining the outcome of elections. Because of the high cost of running for national and state office, we're seeing a rising number of "self-financed" campaigns or candidates who are able to run thanks to a billionaire patron. Each election cycle now features billionaire presidential candidates such as Ross Perot, Steve Forbes, Donald Trump, Michael Bloomberg, Tom Steyer, and Vivek Ramaswany. The 2016 election was dominated by billionaires, with at least one billionaire patron being a requirement for contention.[3] In the 2022 mid-term elections, 44 candidates for federal office spent more than $1 million of their own money to run for office, totaling $221.2 million.[4]

Wealth and Influence. Once candidates are elected, the billionaire class continues to lubricate the political system with ongoing contributions and lobbyists aimed at thwarting any legislation against their interests. Political scientists Benjamin Page and Martin Gilens have written for decades about the disproportionate influence of the wealthy on our political system, especially in their ability to block changes they oppose.[5]

An important takeaway, however, is that money doesn't entirely control the outcome of elections or which policies prevail.[6] Millions spent on negative attack ads don't always work. And sometimes candidates that are independent of the wealthy donor class squeak through and get elected. There is even a negative backlash against self-financed candidates who are perceived as buying their way into office. In the 2022 mid-term congressional elections, only seven of 44 self-financed congressional candidates won their elections. Television doctor Mehmet Oz, who spent $26.8 million of his own money to run for U.S. Senate as a Republican in Pennsylvania, lost to now Democratic Senator John Fetterman.[7]

Sometimes the billionaire donor class is split, financing opposing candidates. Elections become contests between different factions of billionaires, like gladiators sponsored by different monarchs duking it out. In these situations, voters have an opportunity to make a difference. In 2016, the billionaires were lined up behind candidates Hillary Clinton and Donald Trump. But candidate Bernie Sanders, with small campaign contributions averaging $27, remained a vital presence in the race with huge grassroots support. The billionaires don't always win. But they will do everything they can to lower the risk that candidates who don't serve their interests might be elected. The tools in the billionaire political influence toolbox include voter suppression, partisan redistricting, wealth primaries, seeding cynicism, and funding third-party candidates to siphon votes away from challengers.

There are clean election movements pressing a pro-democracy agenda, including stronger campaign finance laws, non-partisan redistricting commissions, full donor disclosures, public financing of elections, and increasing access to the vote.[8] The billionaire donor class will largely oppose reforms that give the non-wealthy a greater voice.

Politics is more than elections. We can join associations and organizations to amplify our voices. We can attend hearings, ask questions, and hold elected officials accountable. And on a couple of important days of the year, we can cast our vote and encourage our family and neighbors to do the same.

Notes

1 Matthew Smith, Owen Zidar, and Eric Zwick, "Top Wealth in America: New Estimates Under Hetergeneous Returns," *Quarterly Journal of Economics*, March 2023, https://zidar.princeton.edu/sites/g/files/toruqf3371/files/documents/wealth2023.pdf.
    Summary: www.economics.princeton.edu/working-papers/top-wealth-in-america-new-estimates-under-heterogenous-returns/.
2 Chuck Collins and Omar Ocampo, "Wealth of US Billionaires Hits $5.5 Trillion, Up 88 percent Since Pandemic Hit," *Common Dreams*, March 18, 2024, https://www.commondreams.org/opinion/billionaire-wealth-explodes-to-5-5-trillion.
3 Kenneth P. Vogel and Isaac Arnsdorf, "The POLITICO 100: Billionaires Dominate 2016," *Politico*, February 8, 2016, https://www.politico.com/story/2016/02/100-billionaires-2016-campaign-finance-218862.
4 Inci Sayki, "Top Self-funding Congressional Candidates Were Election Cycles Biggest Losers," *Open Secrets*, February 13, 2023,
    https://www.opensecrets.org/news/2023/02/top-self-funding-congressional-candidates-were-among-the-2022-midterm-election-cycles-biggest-losers/.
5 Benjamin I. Page and Martin Gilens, *Democracy in America? What Has Gone Wrong and What We Can Do About It* (University of Chicago Press, 2020), https://press.uchicago.edu/ucp/books/book/chicago/D/bo58174159.html.
6 Dylan Matthews, "Remember That Study Saying America Is an Oligarchy? 3 Rebuttals Say Its Wrong," *Vox*, May 9, 2016, https://www.vox.com/2016/5/9/11502464/gilens-page-oligarchy-study.
7 Inci Sayki, "Top Self-funding Congressional Candidates Were Election Cycles Biggest Losers," *Open Secrets*, February 13, 2023,
    https://www.opensecrets.org/news/2023/02/top-self-funding-congressional-candidates-were-among-the-2022-midterm-election-cycles-biggest-losers/.
8 Editorial Board, "More Money, More Problems for Democracy," *The New York Times*, February 1, 2020,
    https://www.nytimes.com/2020/02/01/opinion/sunday/trump-tape-fundraiser.html.

9 The Human Right to Housing

Mary Traynor and Rebecca Garrard

Editors: When it comes to the housing crisis, the mainstream response is that we just have to build more houses and let the market work. Has that worked?

Rebecca Garrard: I think that the argument that supply and demand is the solution to the housing crisis should be one that we can leave behind, and yet we can't seem to be able to. The policies of the last 50 years or so, at local, state, and federal levels, have leaned into that model that if we increase the housing stock, prices will fall. And I think that's true of the arguments for home ownership, for tenants, and for investments on the part of the government. Again, we're talking local, state, and federal, have been driven into that "solution." But all the evidence that we see, from federal opportunity zones to local tax incentives and subsidies to developers, have shown us that despite all of those tax breaks and subsidies for those who create stock, we have seen nothing but an exacerbation – an explosion in fact –of the affordability crisis.

I remain puzzled by how much more evidence we need that increasing supply will solve the crisis, and that leaving the free market to solve the problem without checks and balances is going to be our answer. It's clearly not, and we have to look for other solutions.

Editors: Rebecca, can you give us a sense of the scale of the affordability crisis? What does it look like in terms of numbers? Is it just a few people who are displaced, or is it much worse than that?

Rebecca: There's that statistic that everybody cites: there's no city in the US where a person can work a full-time job that's the minimum wage or the going wage and still fall within the affordability metric in terms of housing. We know that across the country and in every major city, I can certainly speak to New York, over 50% of tenants are rent burdened. And when we say rent burdened, we're using the generally economically acceptable model of what a person's budget should be in terms of housing costs. It should not be more than 30% of your income. We know that

DOI: 10.4324/9781003544371-11

25% to 30% of tenants are severely rent-burdened, which means they're spending over 50% of their income.[1] And so this is not one or two people. This is not one or two cities.

This is a dire crisis. We see the effects of affordability in its most egregious forms in terms of the explosion in the population of those who are unhoused. Our most tragic example of these failed policies is the number of people who are unhoused, again, in New York and across the country, which just continues to skyrocket.

Editors: Mary, can I ask you, if we were to turn to your work in Syracuse, does what Rebecca says ring true to you? Is the situation in Syracuse, which I'm told is now one of the most difficult cities to find a new apartment in, similar to the national picture?

Mary Traynor: Yes, it does. I've been in a couple of meetings here in Syracuse with progressive groups, and I'm there as the Syracuse Tenant Union representative, and people want to talk about supply. I've experienced supply conversations as a way to avoid talking about what we do about people living here in Syracuse *right now.* This is in the terrible housing conditions and unbelievably increased rents *right now* with the landlords they have *now.* People would much rather talk about supply and demand and affordability and formulas and the MRI ["Months of Remaining Inventory"] and all that nonsense, which obviously doesn't work. It's completely broken.

In Syracuse, we tried to get Paul Williams' model of a public developer.[2] It was introduced to our common council, and they replaced the public part of it with Housing Visions and Home Headquarters, which are two not-for-profit housing developers who are as responsible for the housing crisis as anybody else.

On the county level, our county is spending millions and millions of dollars on an aquarium. The reason that vote passed is because one of our Democratic city county reps traded a million dollars to build 10 single-family occupancy new houses in the city. This was hailed as a visionary, bold move. He aligned with the Republicans for this huge project to get 10 single-family houses that people can't afford. But it's just that hole in the market. We need individual people to be able to buy and own single-family homes, and that's going to solve the housing crisis. When that totally doesn't, it has brought us to where we are now. And it's so obvious, it boggles my mind why we think doing more of the same, other than it's capitalism permitting no other models, and capitalism says we need to do more of the same.

And meanwhile, anecdotally, I've heard about a woman who was being evicted in housing court, way past the deadline, who went to the judge, showed her 32 rental applications she had filled out, all of them rejected. I heard of a woman who went to court with 100 rental applications that she had completed, all of them rejected. In those two cases, the judges gave them more time because, what are you going to do? But that's the market at work. And people do not understand that people who are homeless were tenants. The people who are in eviction court getting evicted are the same people who are tomorrow living under the freeway interchange.

Rebecca: This feels so important to me, this whole supply and demand narrative. And there's two things I really want to name. I think of how
housing can't be viewed through a supply and demand model. Let's take
oranges. When there's a bad crop and there's very few oranges, the price
increases. But in the supply and demand capitalist scenario, consumers can always choose not to buy an orange. You can be like, orange is
my favorite fruit, but it's so expensive. I'm going to stick with apples
because it's at my price point.

That is not the case with shelter. When we are talking about something as basic as shelter, there is no apple in this scenario. You will pay anything to be housed, to have a roof over your head. You will forgo healthcare. You will skip a meal that you're feeding your children because there is no apple for shelter. And when people push back against this idea of regulation and infringement, it is always ironic to me because the government has forever regulated utilities. The lights and the heat that we utilize, it's not perfect, but these utilities are highly regulated to keep us warm and keep the lights on. Those things exist in where we're sheltered because they're recognized as such a basic necessity that they cannot be left up to free market will.

And yet, when we talk about that shelter being a basic necessity, in that same vein, we revert to indoctrination around property rights, which is, I am not saying I'd lead with this if I was grassroots organizing because we really need to bring in poor, rural white communities too. But it is so steeped in the roots of our country where property rights were tied to plantations and all of these things, and the country is so indoctrinated that what's really, if you look at it logically and not through this propagandized messaging, should be very simple.

*Editors: Rebecca and Mary, just responding to the points that you've made,
it's clear that there is this dominant model, which is in theory market-
dependent, and has effectively kept people from getting the things they
need. When we think about it in those terms, though, we're often tempted
to thinking about individuals not getting what they need. When we hear
Mary talk about a public developer model, we start imagining something
else, something that's more collective, that society cannot get what it
needs, even more so than this or that individual being deprived – as bad*

as that is. Do you see the public developer model as being feasible if the Right has control over HUD and other federal agencies?

Mary: One pernicious aspect of the conversation about including a public developer is not only can we not subsidize housing, but if we do provide any subsidy for housing, it's seen as taking away from private developers, and that's a bad thing in and of itself. The public developer, as I interpret it, is quite clear. It involves leveraging the state, utilizing the power of the state to issue bonds, and benefiting from lower interest, and the key part being that the state retains control. The argument against it is that, as seen in Syracuse is we need to take care of our not-for-profit developers who are doing a fantastic job here. But, well, it's like, "Well, it'll just turn into the New York City Housing Authority." Of course, the response would be, "Well, okay, there's a couple hundred thousand people who have a roof over their heads, for one thing."

And no. Public developer, as I understand it, has the way it's financially structured in such a way that the ownership remains with the state, which collects management fees, plows that money back into maintenance and infrastructure, and which continue, and then the bonds are paid back. It was designed to be self-sustaining at a high enough level to permit future investment. And it's like the capitalist market is so fragile and defensive, and not only does it not try to do a better job itself, but instead of putting energy into saying, "How can we lower prices so single people can actually afford to buy houses because they can't even do that?", but it puts that energy into attacking any other model as dangerous and doomed to failure.

Editors: Based on how you've just described the public developer model, would a Trump White House and control over HUD make a difference to the feasibility of implementing public developer models?

Mary: Given the authoritarian nature of the Trump policy, and wanting the executive branch to take over all branches of government, it might, right? And given their complete ignorance about how things work. We try to do this on the city level, and we're trying to do it in New York state; there's a proposal. And in the city and the state, we've identified a couple of bonding agencies that could do it. So as far as the effect of Trump on this, well, it's really hard to be convicted of racial discrimination by HUD, and he's done it and his father has done it. So he's really kind of set the bar pretty high for development. He's really not interested in any of this, so I don't think.

Editors: Thanks, Mary. Rebecca, are there policies or old legislation that's worth defending that we should be trying to revive or strengthen in the current system?

Rebecca: It always makes me chuckle out of frustration when we talk about how, "Oh, we don't want to throw good money after bad." Especially when these systems don't go perfectly or need ongoing support. Because when we had the banking crisis, let's all remember, nobody minded at all, throwing billions and billions of dollars at the wealthiest banks to stabilize their poor choices, I would assert, right? And boy, that phrase is leveraged at poor people all the time, right? Their poor choices, their bad financial decisions. Nobody blinked; that money went out the door in a hot second.

There was no means testing. All of a sudden, there were billions and billions of dollars to throw at the problem. But when we're talking about the ones who are the least well off, the blame and shame assigning increases dramatically, as does our assessment of whether you are worthy of investment. I always take umbrage at how much more justification you have to do for the investment of public money for public good when we're talking about the people who actually should be first in line to receive it.

Since Mary brought up the New York City Housing Authority (NYCHA), I want to talk about public housing because it was actually very successful and could have remained very successful, if it weren't for the policies that derailed it, right? We know that when public housing was first created, it was in the early 1900s, and it was for white people, and it was well-funded, robustly funded, and highly successful. However, when the Fair Housing Act was passed and desegregation started being required, the defunding of public housing was immediate and drastic. What we have are these examples that are often cited as abysmal failures, such as NYCHA, to show how public housing models don't work. We only need to look back to earlier instances in this country to see how well they worked. We certainly can look at European cities to see how well they work.

The ones that don't work were because of very intentional and very swift disinvestment. And so I think one thing we should do and should have done a long time ago is, when we've spent the last 50 years throwing money at developers, we should be investing in publicly owned or operated housing that stays affordable in perpetuity. And in my mind, we can start to talk about adding to that, what would our housing crisis look like if we just said all the money that we're diverting into wealthy developers and we diverted it into the creation of publicly operated, publicly owned, affordable in perpetuity structures, that in and of itself, would make a tremendous difference.

Editors: Makes sense to us. Rebecca, if we may put the same question that I put to Mary to you: assuming we have a change in administration in the direction of the right, of Trump, where do you see your work going, and what are the problems that may arise?
Rebecca: I mean, it's terrifying, and I'm not being hyperbolic.

I think if we're just talking about Biden through the lens of housing policy, some of the policies that he's putting forth are some of the best policies we've seen from a president, if I'm being totally honest, around housing in recent history. He's talking about things that haven't been talked about, like limiting and capping rents for buildings that have federally backed loans. That's huge.

If we pivot to a Trump presidency, we are talking about, I think, not just losing momentum toward additional rights for small homeowners and tenants, but we're talking about a gutting of the rights that already exist. I think we're talking about incentives and subsidies being maintained and created for the wealthiest developers.

We're not talking about the small family who wants to transition from tenant to homeowner. We're talking about your BlackRocks; we're talking about your private equity firms, both domestic and abroad, that are slowly and methodically acquiring the housing stock in this country. That being made easier and happening more rapidly. It is imperative that people understand the very real and very immediate consequences of that vote in November on their very direct material living conditions.

Editors: Mary, if we were to turn back to you, given the scenario that Rebecca has painted here, how would your organizing change after November if the right were to come back to power? We know that in the day-to-day organizing work, we are dealing with very specific problems: lead, mold, et cetera, right? Or the inability to make rent for this particular month or the rent going up. But how would we be able to introduce conversations about the larger political situation in that context?

Mary: Right now, a lot of people in Syracuse are seeing their rents go up 50% from 800 to 1,200. While their incomes are not going up at all, they're working two part-time jobs and trying to take the bus. So that's going to be increasing. I think that at least on the local level, our collegial approach and our offers to government officials, both elected and administrative, along with all our ideas for improving conditions, have been dismissed. We have been trying to just increase protections, and there's been this ongoing background effort to get the Emergency Tenant Protection Act actually enacted, which would impact a very small percentage of people and building owners. I really think people are going to be more ready to take some kind of direct action.

I'm talking about city-wide rent strikes, clogging up and shutting down housing courts, camping out in front of these developers' homes, because they all live in homes in the white suburbs, beautiful big homes. I think people will be more ready for that because our niceness has failed, been rejected utterly, and this is what's happened. Things are exponentially worse. I don't know what the effect will be, but I'm getting really, really sick of being nice to people and trying to have meetings with them because it's not working. There's kind of this financial analysis of the percentage of rent and rent burden and stuff. What I'm seeing kind of pushing people and trying to get into conversations with our elected officials and people who run neighborhood business development, code enforcement, there is a suspicion of, it is such a class-bound thing.

It's Black women with a bunch of kids who are tenants, and they are scary, right? People are frightened: people, white people, people who own property, and people who solicit votes and money from the real estate sector. Both the big real estate lobby and the small landlords here in Syracuse play on that fear. They support that fear through criminal background checks. And it is just that the whole conversation switches, and tenants are so much a part of this. I think trying to talk nicely and enter into dialogue and have a good discussion; it takes two. It takes both sides to do that. I have come to the belief since 2018 that they really don't care and don't want to listen. Tenants have not united strongly enough and still kind of buy into that individualist ethos of "We just have to work harder, and my tenant neighbor upstairs is a bad person." I think people are seeing, like, okay, my rent went up 50%. What am I going to do? The judge won't even evict me. I don't know what will happen. I don't know what that will look like, but I hope it'll be a lot more aggressive on the streets.

Editors: Clearly, what we're hearing from you is that there might be an electoral component to our work, but our issues and our agenda go well beyond elections to a whole other set of terrains as well. Nonetheless, we want to ask Rebecca, if we were to think of, say, a young person, a tenant who's okay – they can afford to pay their rent, they're in okay housing and all – and they have a sense that there's a problem with the way housing is administered right now, how would you suggest they get involved? What are the kinds of organizations they can look to, one, get educated, but also look to in order to begin to take action?

Rebecca: There are lots of grassroots organizations in our state and across the country. I think they should choose ones, to be honest, that are very good at lifting up the voices of people who are impacted by the crisis, because let's start at the most extreme end of the scale of the housing crisis. The narrative around the unhoused is that they're lazy or they're criminals.

If you ever spent time talking to people who were unhoused, the vast majority of them lived a very normal, typical life until that one tragedy that the vast majority of us are only a paycheck away from sent them down a path they couldn't recover from. I think it's important for people who feel stable and feel outside of that cycle of housing and security to understand that *no one is*, that it's one health accident or incident, it's one job layoff, it's one crisis like that that can put anyone in that cycle. There are so many organizations working on this that I don't want to prioritize one over the other, but we should support the kind of organization that enables people can see themselves in the problem even if they're not immediately experiencing it.

This is an issue that resonates across party lines. The problem is that the real estate industry and the wealthy do a very good job of pitting impacted people against each other. It's their recipe for success. I have to worry about getting mine, so I'm in competition with you. Whether that's along racial lines, ethnic lines, or rural/urban lines, you name it. But capitalism and free market housing survive and thrive on, it depends on it. And yet when we organize in white rural communities, that housing insecurity resonates in the same way as when we organize in Black urban communities, in the South, in the North, or in the North or the Midwest. So, what we need to do a better job of is not having that organizing happen in silos and buckets but creating more of a coalescing of those groups.

I think New York has been a great model for that in our statewide coalition. We have miles to go before we sleep and a tremendous amount of progress in connecting upstate New York with western New York and with New York City. Without that happening on a broader scale, we won't have the unity we need to effect that change. And I think that has to be part of the organizing conversation. This has to be an electoral conversation.

I mean, I still knock on doors, and I hear, what has the government done for me? What people have to understand is that's so valid. I usually phrase it as, "And I'm asking you to take this leap of faith with me." Change starts now with this engagement. What I know is we can't change it with the people who are in office. What I believe is that we can with someone else who's accountable to you, not to their real estate donors. And I'm asking you to take that leap of faith. It doesn't always work, but it works sometimes. And I do love the radical rent strikes; it's all part of the puzzle. It almost has to almost all happen simultaneously.

Editors: Mary, do you have any observations on this particular point?
Mary: In the Syracuse Tenant Union, we get calls from individuals in the counties, in outlying areas in the county where there's nothing. A lot of places don't even have code enforcement. They're calling about their specific problem, and we can tell them the state law that's applicable to that specific problem. We could so easily turn that into a really powerful political conversation and tell people, "Your problems, white rural person, are the same as a Black person on the south side. Why is that?" Almost in a sense, using people's housing crises to shine a light on the underlying political commonalities that can really change things.

I mean, on a local level, we got a housing judge elected. It was a very intentional electoral campaign. She is gutting landlords. It's like years of frustration about housing conditions and tenants, and she is absolutely blowing our minds. I just couldn't believe it. She's just being fair. She's giving tenants their day in court. It really matters. We have a good senator. It really matters.

Again, people do not see themselves as playing any role in government at all. People don't know the difference between city and county government. But given that there's a blank slate, we can fill in the blanks. Because people know with their bodies how bad things are. One thing I was going to say … I used to do foreclosure defense. So these are homeowners. Most people had been tenants, and they were in a home, and they couldn't believe that one paycheck, one radiator, a $300 car bill was resulting in this because they were a homeowner, and therefore everything was going to be okay. They were never going to have to rent again. They had made it. They were no longer that kind of person who rented. They had entered this whole different class. You fall down and you break your ankle, that's it. You're losing your house six months later. And so, we have to organize across the divides of renter and homeowner too.

Editors: Your answer and Rebecca's last point really provide us with a sense of some inspiration, hearing that against the realtor and developer interest in dividing populations, there are, in fact, commonalities of experience that we can turn to and perhaps knit together into a new narrative about housing and our right to housing.

Notes

1 Joint Center for Housing Studies of Harvard University, *America's Rental Housing* (Cambridge, MA: Harvard University, January 2024), https://www.jchs.harvard .edu/sites/default/files/reports/files/Harvard_JCHS_Americas_Rental_Housing _2024.pdf.
2 Paul E. Williams, "Carving out a Path for Public Developers," *Substack Newsletter, Social Housing Chronicle* (blog), July 14, 2022, https://housingchronicle.substack .com/p/carving-out-a-path-for-public-developers.

10 Holding the Fort, Birthing a New World – or Why Labor Unions Matter

Ben Manski

I have been asked to deliver a kind of monologue on the role of labor unions in the search for a good society. I'll begin by stating that I've been a union member for 35 years. I've been active in unions as a rank-and-file member, as a steward, as an officer, and as support staff, in five different union locals in the AFT, NEA, and UAW as well as in the IWW. Members of my family have been involved in unions for at least a century. I've never known a time when unions were not a part of my life, and so I find it difficult to imagine a social movement from which unions are absent.

What I know and see is that labor unions are vital to two tasks in this long period in which the world system is in terminal crisis. Unions are capable of defending the republican promise of a government of the people and for the people. And unions are increasingly providing leadership in bringing government by the people – democracy – into our economy and into our relationships with the rest of nature. To paraphrase two legendary labor songs, unions today can both "Hold the Fort" and, at the same time, help "bring to birth a new world from the ashes of the old."

I see the power of today's union movement all around me. But even so, others don't. A common view is shaped by the question of how many workers belong to unions today as opposed to 80 years ago. This is often described as the problem of union density, and it goes like this: because the percentage of workers who belong to labor unions in the US has hit somewhere between 10 and 11% of the formal workforce, down from a height of more than 30% a couple of generations ago, unions are no longer able to force the boss class to compromise.

That argument has a lot to it. It is certainly the case that historically, in the mid-20th century, unions were foundational for the broader social movement in the United States. The strength of union organizations and the resources they were able to mobilize meant that all kinds of other possibilities emerged far beyond factory walls and union halls. The bosses had to come to the table to strike bargains with working people – bargains that went by names like "The New Deal" and "The Great Society." Those bargains were the bargains

DOI: 10.4324/9781003544371-12

that people of my parents' generation and their parents' generation grew up with, and they treated those bargains as normal.

For this reason, as unions lost membership precipitously, and as unions were driven out of their close relationships with government agencies and the managers of our major institutions, many people of the 1930s and 1960s generations concluded that this meant that the labor movement was no longer going to be as central as it had been to the project of social change. For many of them, this meant that the possibility of the United States becoming some form of a social democracy – something that not only seemed possible in the late 1970s but which I believe really was (for better or for worse) possible – was no longer on the table. What we've seen since the 1970s is that the earlier normalcy of the social contract between capital and labor has proven to have been the exception in American history. The Cold War period was an aberration, not the rule. Thus, I agree that the decline in union membership means that unions will not play the same role they might have played when I was born.

But having said that, it remains true that, as they were prior to the Cold War period, unions are incredibly important organizations for achieving real democracy.

Let's remember, to begin with, that it was in the periods in which unions were illegal and in which violence against organized workers was at its greatest level – replete with massacres, mass deportations, blacklists, and mass imprisonment of labor activists – that the labor movement built and wielded its greatest power. The right to vote, municipal home rule, public education, direct election of U.S. Senators, direct legislation, social security, and a host of workplace safety, child labor, working hour, wage, and other economic justice laws were won by a labor movement facing what Jack London called "The Iron Heel" of the capitalist state.

Today, as we're in a period in which (at least for the moment) we're not experiencing anything close to those levels of repression, unions are approaching levels of creativity, dynamism, and inclusivity more similar to the leading edges of the labor movement more than a century ago than to the unions of the Cold War period. We are seeing again what the United Farm Workers and Marshall Ganz have taught us about strategic capacity: It's not the resources that unions hoard that make them powerful, it's their resourcefulness in what they do that makes unions powerful.

Today we are seeing the fruits of a union reform movement that began in the 1970s, just as union membership was beginning to collapse. That movement struggled with the ossified and often corrupt union bureaucracies of the past, fought to democratize unions, and led the way toward a union movement that advocates and strikes for all working people regardless of gender, sexuality, ethnicity, nationality, race, age, ability, economic sector, or location in the world system. That movement has worked to make unions social again: to build unions that fight for society, not just their members.

Since the late 1990s, we've been seeing signs of the reform movement's success. We saw it with the fight against NAFTA, the UPS Strike of 1997, and the Seattle Uprising against the World Trade Organization. We saw it with the May Day "Day Without an Immigrant" in 2006 and the participation of many unions in the immigrant rights and anti-war movements of the 2000s. We saw it again on a massive scale with the Wisconsin Uprising of 2011, and then the participation of unions in Occupy Wall Street and Occupy everywhere. We saw unions grappling with police brutality and white supremacy and deciding what side they were on as tens of millions declared that Black Lives Matter. We saw general strikes and wildcat strikes in public education from Chicago to California and West Virginia to Oklahoma. We saw the railroad unions prepare for a national strike to demand public ownership of the railroads. And this past year, we've seen a new UAW promising to "Unite All Workers for Democracy," winning massive strikes, organizing auto workers across the South, and inspiring nearly 5,000 union activists gathered at the latest Labor Notes conference in Chicago.

This is a very different union movement than that of my parents' generation. Popular support for unions has doubled to 70% compared to what it was when they were my age. How could this movement not fill me with optimism? Yes, union density is down. But union power is up.

Power to do what? I'll start to address that by taking on another knock on union power. It's often pointed out that union density would be much lower were it not for the growth of unions in the public sector. This criticism reminds me of Republican staffers in my home state of Wisconsin who would claim that "if it weren't for Madison and Milwaukee, Wisconsin would be a conservative state." Putting aside the fact that Wisconsin is filled with progressive rural communities, not just urban ones, my response was always, "Madison and Milwaukee couldn't exist anywhere other than Wisconsin." The same holds true for the public sector: The US has a public sector, needs a public sector, and wouldn't be the US without a public sector.

Beyond this and more to the point: The fact that unions have so much power in the public sector matters because it is public institutions that we rely on for so many of the strategies for achieving economic and political democracy in this country. For example, if you're working to build community wealth by bringing together major anchor institutions to deploy their resources to develop local economic systems filled with worker-owned businesses, cooperatives, community services, land trusts, social housing, local exchange, and the like, then you are relying on institutions that are unionized. Whether we're talking about Richmond, Virginia or Richmond, California, unions matter in local governments, hospitals, universities, and the other major institutions that anchor economic development. This means that unions in general, and public sector unions in particular, matter for community wealth building.

Another place where unions matter is in building cooperatives. This is new, or at least, new in a back-to-the-future kind of way. Just as the railroad and farmers' unions of Eugene V. Debs' daydreamed of a North American "Cooperative Commonwealth," today the union movement is finally getting past its 20th-century addiction to state-sponsored collective bargaining and beginning to back worker and community ownership. I'd seen glimmers of this shift in various places in recent years. But we saw evidence for this change all over the place at the Labor Notes 2024 conference, with case after case of electrical workers, carpenters, pipefitters, auto workers, nurses, machinists, professors, railroaders – you name it – building hybrid union cooperatives or mobilizing for public ownership. This trend is especially strong among those working to speed the transition to renewable energy and a climate-safe future.[1] As *The New Republic's* Katie Myers recently wrote, "UAW's Latest Labor Victory Is a Huge Climate Win, Too."[2]

This is not happenstance. It's happening because of a lot of smart, hard work that people of different backgrounds and generations in unions, the environmental movement, and community organizations have done together. Let's give a special shout-out to the Labor Network for Sustainability and the U.S. Federation of Worker Cooperatives. Those folks are doing incredible work.

Now, I have spoken in general terms, with a kind of overview. Let me begin to close with a list of examples worth further exploration. To start, I'll return to Railroad Workers United and the recent votes to authorize a national railroad strike. Union reformers within the rail sector, coordinated across 13 different unions by Railroad Workers United, building over decades, were successful not only in bringing all of their unions together to vote to strike, but also in coming together around the demand for public ownership of the railroads. Congress and Biden stepped in to outlaw the strike. But the railroaders' campaign for public ownership is ongoing. I expect it will continue to resonate across other sectors of American society in a significant way.

There are a number of innovative examples of IBEW union locals moving forward for renewable energy. In Wisconsin, for example, utilities signed on with IBEW, North Central States Regional Council of Carpenters, the Wisconsin Laborers' District Council, and the Wisconsin Operating Engineers 139, to work on an anticipated 100 new renewable energy projects in the coming decade. These will generate and store some 16 gigawatts of energy annually.[3] In the Southwest, IBEW signed a project labor agreement to build a $1.3 billion, 580-mile transmission that will connect 3.5 gigawatts of wind power to communities across the region.[4] In the Northeast, in Massachusetts and New York, you find the IBEW coming to terms with public ownership and energy alternatives.[5]

At the level of organizational innovation and creating new economic relationships, I refer readers to Rebecca Lurie and Bernadette Fitzsimons's excellent "A Union Toolkit for Cooperative Solutions."[6] In it, readers and activists will find accounts and analysis of some of the inspiring work that today's unions are involved with. One case they document is that of Co-op Dayton, a non-profit formed to address food apartheid. Its earliest investments came from labor unions. Their support included providing a union staffer dedicated to devoting her efforts to forming a coop. Labor movement support also helped mobilize the public to get local governments behind the coop.

In another exciting example, rank-and-file members of IBEW Local 3 formed the People's Choice Communications Cooperative (PCCC), a multi-stakeholder coop uniting workers, consumers, and under-resourced communities. They seized the restructuring of the cable industry as an opportunity to build their coop. When an expanded Time-Warner Cable corporation was acquired and rebranded as part of Spectrum Cable in 2017, unionized workers came under attack, with cuts to their healthcare, retirement, and other benefits. Moreover, the company refused to bargain in good faith. More than 1,800 unionized technicians went on strike. The company replaced the striking workers and eventually, in 2022, the five-year-long strike was officially called off. However, the workers went on to form a cooperative offering internet connectivity to low-income communities at a critical time: during the pandemic. While PCCC has had mixed results and had to deal with (often corrupt) competition from the for-profit corporate sector for access to public housing contracts, it nonetheless demonstrates a new face of labor – one for community empowerment and cutting across the worker-consumer divide.

In their work, Lurie and Fitzsimmons identify seven key, though not always obvious, elements that labor unions bring to the cooperative and economic justice movement. Foremost among these is an "openness to innovative organizing" (which to me also means democracy) – a readiness to engage new voices within the union or the broader community. Secondly, unions have professional expertise and paid staff. A third element is that unions have facilities, physical spaces, and communications that are vital but often lacking in under-resourced communities. Fourth, unions have training funds; under some circumstances, these can be leveraged to access federal and state workforce development funds. A fifth element is access to capital that can leverage access to financial institutions for the benefit of communities. In their routine operations, trade unions develop expertise in a sixth element – negotiations. This too can be deployed to assist communities and cooperatives. The seventh element involves the awareness that unions develop as they organize, expand, and bargain, about the socioeconomic sector in which they operate; this kind of sectoral analysis of everything from supply chains to the environmental context to legislative politics can benefit workers in coops and the broader community.

All in all, it is the resourcefulness of unions in what they do, not the resources that they hoard, that makes them powerful. Forging a new compromise with the bosses? Yes, maybe that's off the table. Instead, unions are DIYing it – doing it themselves – and in the process, playing a vital role in making possible a next system beyond the bosses.

Maybe that's just too much happy talk for some? Okay, I'll humor you.

For another system to be possible, it must not only be born but also live long enough to become resilient. This is where "holding the fort" comes in. Unions today are by far the strongest organizations in the United States capable of defending voting rights and the promise of democratic elections. They have shown time and again that they can bring numbers, organization, discipline, solidarity, and technical expertise into the fray. No other social movement organizations come remotely close.

Now let's turn to our current moment. At the beginning of this decisive decade, the Republic was preserved in a shocking way. It survived because on January 6, 2021, civic republicanism proved to be alive in the U.S. armed forces. Officers and enlisted personnel both refused to participate in a fascist coup. In the final analysis, nothing else stood in the way. If in 2024 the US military remains the last bastion against a repeat of January 6, the prospects for a next system that's better than our current one become much worse.

During the American Revolution, the emergence of a professional military was regarded as "the bane of liberty." I'm glad that civic honor and a sense of republicanism are alive in the US military. But today's labor unions are a much better bet if we're to hold the fort long enough for new forms of democracy to gain strength.

Union density may be down, but union power? It's there when it's most needed.

Notes

1 "2024 Labor Notes Conference: April 19–21," *Labor Notes*, November 8, 2023, https://labornotes.org/2024.
2 April 28, 2024, https://newrepublic.com/article/180958/uaw-volkswagen-chatta-nooga-just-transition.
3 Erik Gunn, "Wisconsin Electric Utilities Sign on to Union Labor for Clean Energy Projects • Wisconsin Examiner," *Wisconsin Examiner* (blog), March 24, 2024, https://wisconsinexaminer.com/briefs/wisconsin-electric-utilities-sign-on-to-union -labor-for-clean-energy-projects/.
4 Matt Spence, "IBEW Signs Agreement for Largest Renewable Energy Project in North American History," *IBEW Media Center*, December 13, 2023, https://ibew .org/media-center/Articles/23Daily/2312/RenewableEnergyProject.
5 See A.J. Ruther in this collection on Public Power in New York.
6 Rebecca Lurie and Bernadette King Fitzsimmons, *A Union Toolkit for Cooperative Solutions* (New York: The Community and Worker Ownership Project at the CUNY School of Labor and Urban Studies, Autumn 2021), https://drive.google.com/file/d /1pl7154R4_XHY3qTzRlPxpHPS30kK9b-e/view.

11 A Union for All Workers

Mike Miller

Editors: Recently, UAW President Shawn Fain described the working class as "the arsenal of democracy." Can you tease that out a little bit for us? What does it mean for the current election, especially that of 2024?

Mike Miller: For context, it's a reference to Franklin Delano Roosevelt, who in 1940 referred to working people as the arsenal of democracy. The specific referent was the Ford Motor Company aircraft factory at Willow Run, just outside of Detroit. They built the B-24 Liberator bomber that had an outsized role in fighting the Nazis in Europe. And that was a United Auto Workers-represented plant. World War II saw a popular front formation that really helped propel the US labor movement forward in important ways. It saw a quasi-industrial policy that reflected the growing strength of the US labor movement. It won important concessions to the labor movement in exchange for labor peace and in an effort to beat fascism globally. It was an imperfect agreed compromise at the time. But it is sort of apt because we find ourselves in an imperfect position now, in the current conjuncture going into the election in November 2024 for the upcoming electoral cycle from a worker's perspective and a working-class movement perspective.

You have a number of candidates whom the UAW has endorsed and is supporting, who are imperfect from a working-class perspective. Indeed, far from perfect, but they represent a better alternative than who's likely to be the other candidate given our electoral system. It's just important that we use every avenue, every mechanism of power that we can as a movement – a worker's movement – to try to build power for working people in this country and across the globe.

The fact that the Biden administration is attempting to have a worker-centered industrial policy with the transition to a green economy is important. The Biden administration recognizes that climate change is real and that fossil fuels lead to climate change and the injustices created by it. The administration is developing a worker-centered industrial policy that seeks to address

DOI: 10.4324/9781003544371-13

climate change in more socially and environmentally just ways. It's imperfect, but it's starting to move in the right direction.

I don't think it's a secret that almost half of our membership in the union, especially in the auto sector, voted for Trump in the last election. We really need to show leadership to mobilize voters to vote for as many progressive pro-working-class candidates. This will help create a governing mandate in the upcoming elections.

Editors: You talk about the need to show leadership and, in many ways, the progressives and the rest of the world are looking at the UAW again – much as they did in the 1980s in its fight against apartheid South Africa, in the 1950s and 1960s with Civil Rights, or in the 1930s. And of course, with the recent victory in the South, in Chattanooga, TN. In some ways, you personify the resurrection of the UAW, right? After all, you helped organize a labor union outside of the traditional area of focus of the UAW in the 1990s, brought tens of thousands of workers into the UAW. How do you understand and describe the rebirth of the UAW as a leading moral and political force?

Mike: That's a good question. It has been a long time coming. In the 1990s, when we were initially involved in organizing at our workplace at UCLA, we took a lot of inspiration from what autoworkers had been able to accomplish in the 1930s and 1940s, and then, as you say, in the 1980s, fighting apartheid. So, our movement was inspired by the autoworkers movement. Certainly, in Region 6, which has been one of the most progressive parts of the UAW when it still existed prior to its recent reincarnation, and certainly within the direction of Paul Schrade and his opposition to the Vietnam War, his support for the United Farm Workers Union and for civil and immigrant rights more generally.[1]

We certainly drew on that, but we also had to come up with our own organizing practices and strategies. Unions weren't super prevalent at universities at the time – and certainly not for student workers. Labor law in both the private sector and the public sector was organized against us. It excluded us as if we weren't really workers and didn't have the right to bargain collectively. And so, we had to fight. We had to organize, we had to strike. Also, at the time in the 1990s when we were getting started, you had a lot of right-wing political attacks on unions in general, whether it was Proposition 187 that sought to criminalize undocumented immigrants or Proposition 209 that sought to do away with affirmative action. These were all different fights that we were engaged in but that we saw as interrelated and connected. The opposition to the first Persian Gulf War led to the Radical Students Alliance and the Network for Public Education and Social Justice, out of which the union movement and related networks helped to birth the union at UCLA.

Those were all important and related struggles. Then we won recognition from the University of California. In many ways, as the UAW leadership took a bad turn and sank into the depths of corruption and bureaucracy, we had to fight against our own union as well, and do that delicately and creatively, using some of the same tactics that we had learned and developed in fighting the University of California. At the same time, we were seeking to grow the union and the part of the union that was organizing and fighting for social justice more broadly. By doing that, we were able to, with the support of our siblings throughout the organization and the country, fight to have a one member, one vote as a mechanism for choosing the leaders of the union. I think this opened many possibilities to not only elect different people but to have more freedom to do things that, as a union, were more militant, aimed at organizing the whole working class, and had a more politically progressive focus.

Editors: We're most impressed with the idea of a two-front struggle – struggling for reform within the union, while at the same time expanding the union. Often, we have gone for one front over the other, and as a result, we get no reform because we concentrate on dutifully expanding the union, or we focus on fighting the leadership and it just becomes an internecine war. But you seem to have found the balance there.

Mike: Yes, it is challenging because, on the one hand, you have to fight to reform the union internally, but sometimes the story of this struggle is seized upon by the anti-union forces in society and is used to stop you from growing as a movement. They say, "Look, do you want to be involved in this kind of food fight or circular firing squad," or whatever metaphor they're going to use to paint it in a negative light. So, yes, it is a challenge.

Editors: Are there any lessons that you have for how to conduct such a subtle and nuanced kind of engagement – how to make sure that it does not appear like a circular firing squad? Certainly, your example of the reform – a direct election of officers on a one member, one vote model – -seems to be one very positive example. It seems like a story you can tell both to members as well as to the general public.

Mike: I think that was a good tactic. There is also a point about how we comported ourselves: being very disciplined about continuing to organize. Together with other leaders, we made a commitment to each other to keep organizing, to keep bringing new people into the union, and to keep being creative about how to do that. In itself, this organizing was an act of reform because it was very much opposed by people in power who didn't want new people with new ideas and new energy to come into the union. In and of itself, it both pushed the reform agenda and, because it gave us more votes, more power to act on our reform agenda, and it did the thing we were all about, which is building more powerful working people in society at the same time.

Editors: That certainly makes sense. From your vantage point within the leadership of the UAW, looking out at the broader labor movement and broader democracy movement, what's your sense of what our priorities need to be?

Mike: Last night [April 24, 2024], a number of our leaders at the University of Southern California were arrested by the Los Angeles Police Department for protesting in favor of a ceasefire in Gaza, and protesting the US's role in supporting the genocide that's taking place there. I do think that that's a very glaring and immediate issue that is at the front of all our minds, and it relates to the presidential election. I don't know that the Democratic Party's nominee is going to be able to win if they don't do more to call for and to effectuate a ceasefire. And not just a ceasefire, but more humanitarian aid to Gaza and occupied territories, less military aid, no military aid, stop spending our tax dollars on weapons, giving weapons to people who are committing genocide. I think those are immediate pressing issues.[2]

There are also critical union organizing drives – the election in Tennessee at the Volkswagen plant, and the one coming soon in Alabama at the Mercedes plant.[3] We are continuing to organize in the higher education sector. I believe we have 32,000 workers who are in the process of bargaining for a first contract right now. And that movement is growing with greater speed. We have a big contract negotiation in the heavy truck sector of the union in the Carolinas that might go on strike very soon. So, all those things are priorities, but especially growing the labor movement, getting the most pro-union people elected, pro-worker, pro-working-class people elected in the upcoming election as possible, and then really fighting for our agenda.

Elections are just moments in time when leaders are selected. We then need to hold those leaders accountable in order to have, I would say, a foreign policy that reflects the interests of the working class globally, whether that's immigration reform. It is just beyond problematic that capital flows freely across borders, but workers can't – and that we criminalize and vilify people who are coming to the United States because of the incredible poverty and violence that they're experiencing in their own country because of *our* economic and foreign policies. We need to do much better on that. We need to do much better on the trillions of dollars we spend on the military and the way that's applied throughout the world. There's a lot that we must do to address climate change.

Editors: There is a tough question then, right? Given all these different priorities, for example, how do we win a majority of UAW members to the position that there needs to be a ceasefire in Gaza? Or that we must expand humanitarian aid, or a just political solution. How do we conduct those conversations?

Mike: I think it's by looking, talking to people, having members and workers talk to each other. People from the labor movement in Gaza and the occupied territories talk to workers here about what they're experiencing. It really pierces through to actually talk to real people. It's harder to be like, "Israel's God's country, and so we have to support it." Talking to someone whose house was bombed by weapons that are made by your union siblings in the United States and paid for with your tax dollars – I think that's an important thing.

I see that we're doing some solidarity work with independent auto worker unions in Mexico right now, and the delegations of leaders from those unions who've come to the US, and they sit down with ... I think the GM plant in Silao, Mexico makes the same truck that we make at two different plants, one in Indiana, one in Michigan, and then another plant in Canada. And to all sit down and talk to each other, all the workers at those different plants, and see that the production's the same, the vehicle's the same. It is sold for the same amount of money. But the wages that the workers make and the conditions in which they make those trucks are totally different.[4] And coming to terms with that reality is powerful, powerful, powerful. It overcomes whatever xenophobic or racist ideas that may be on the surface of someone's consciousness.

Editors: What is very hopeful in your account is that within the structure of the union there is the capacity to conduct these direct conversations and to achieve a consciousness that breaks through the media blockades and other forms of, for want of a better word, ideological hegemony, right?

Mike: Absolutely. It's harder to get workers' union leaders from Palestine to come here. But in Detroit and in New Jersey, we have huge concentrations of members who are Palestinian or Arab American, who work in auto factories. Having one of those union members who can talk about these issues is vital. Some of our best leaders come from that background, and they can talk to other members about it. And it is powerful!

Editors: How do people who are not in the labor movement relate to or get involved in solidarity with the UAW and its campaigns?

Mike: They can organize as part of the UAW! They can reach out to us. We sometimes joke that UAW means union for all workers. Reach out! We are happy to help any group of workers who wants to organize.

Other ways: You can be involved in politics wherever you live. You can get in touch with your central labor council.[5] Every county has a central labor council.

Notes

1   See Nelson Lichtenstein and Harold Meyerson, "The Autoworker Who Transformed California - The American Prospect," *The American Prospect*, November 25, 2022,

https://prospect.org/labor/autoworker-who-transformed-california-paul-schrade-obit/.

2 See Chris Skelly, "UAW Statement on Israel and Palestine," *UAW | United Automobile, Aerospace and Agricultural Implement Workers of America* (blog), December 1, 2023, https://uaw.org/uaw-statement-israel-palestine/.

3 [Editors: A few days after the interview, the union lost the representation election by 597 votes out of some 5,000 cast. The UAW is contesting the election outcome, pointing to labor law violations by management. See Jeremy Kimbrell, "Lessons from the UAW's Alabama Mercedes Loss," *Jacobin*, May 22, 2024, https://jacobin.com/2024/05/uaw-alabama-mercedes-union-loss.]

4 See the statement by the Secretary of Labor on the collective bargaining agreement won by workers in Silao: Marty Walsh, "Vote by Workers at GM's Silao, Mexico Auto Plant to Approve Collective Bargaining Agreement," *Department of Labor*, June 1, 2022, https://www.dol.gov/newsroom/releases/osec/osec20220601-0.

5 "State Federations and Central Labor Councils | AFL-CIO," accessed June 2, 2024, https://aflcio.org/about-us/our-unions-and-allies/state-federations-and-central-labor-councils.

12 Flow of Resistance

The Power of Border Communities Shaping America's Future

Matt Nelson and Nancy Treviño

Nestled along the banks of the Rio Grande lies Eagle Pass, Texas – a community defined by its resilience, diversity, and unwavering spirit. For generations, Eagle Pass has been a beacon of hope for migrants seeking refuge and a symbol of solidarity and cultural power amidst a recent landscape marked by incredible adversity.

As the border militarization escalates, residents of Eagle Pass find themselves grappling with a surreal sense of dissonance. For Robie Flores, a filmmaker deeply rooted in the community, the disparity between reality and memory is stark.

> I look at images of my home that we've captured over the last six years, and it still resembles the place I've known my entire life. Yet, when I return home after work and see the current state of affairs depicted in the news or in photos shared by friends and family, I feel like I'm witnessing a foreign world. It resembles a war zone, starkly contrasting with the familiar scenes I've grown up with.

While the physical landscape changes, the emotional and psychological toll of border militarization intensifies. As a member of the Eagle Pass Border Coalition, Flores is intimately acquainted with the community's resilience, its context, and hopes for the future.

In 2021, Texas Governor Greg Abbott launched Operation Lone Star (OLS), a militarized, discriminatory border initiative meant to address the increase of migrants arriving at the U.S.-Mexico border in search of protection.[1]

Since its implementation, Human Rights Watch has documented its detrimental effects, including racial profiling, violations of migrant and asylum seeker rights, and suppression of freedoms, reporting that "the program has led to injuries and deaths, increased racial profiling of border residents, consistently violated the rights of migrants and asylum seekers as well as US citizens, and suppressed freedom of association and expression."[2] All in all, OLS

DOI: 10.4324/9781003544371-14

has been disastrous, and as Governor Abbott's antics have persisted, he has zeroed in on Eagle Pass, Texas, which has become the epicenter of his hate.

Solidarity Is Greater than Hate

Faced with the prospect of razor buoys in the Rio Grande and militarization of their beloved Shelby Park, residents and their allies chose to fight back. Led by local activists and filmmakers, the rapidly growing Eagle Pass Border Coalition and Border Vigil organized marches, press conferences, and vigils to raise awareness about the devastating impact of Abbott's policies.[3] This growing movement of Latine leaders on the U.S.-Mexico border flexing their political power is indicative of how much the border matters in shaping policy priorities and winning elections.

Governor Abbott's rhetoric and policies are an all too familiar echo of former President Trump's hate speech that has inspired the spread of "great replacement" conspiracy theories and "invasion" rhetoric. Disastrously, elected officials have upped the ante by repeating these lies,[4] causing fear in Latine communities of an increase in hate crimes against our families.[5] But the region has inspired our communities to organize, reframe the border narrative, and build political power to ensure elected officials and candidates are voted out and held accountable.

Eagle Pass Border Coalition member Jessie F. Fuentes says:

> Our beautiful and safe public park has been taken away from us, and turned into a military style staging area, now being used as a backdrop for political theater by Governor Abbott, who lives over 200 miles away, and out-of-state politicians. Even the TV celebrity Dr. Phil, who lives in Beverly Hills, CA has been allowed into our park. Meanwhile, local residents can no longer use our park for fishing, kayaking, flea markets, sports, barbecues, quinceañeras, or to have our children play, as we did daily for generations.

In an open letter to Governor Abbott, Fuentes called on Governor Abbott to relinquish control over Shelby Park, a public space that has been inaccessible to residents since January 19, 2024.

The contested U.S.-Mexico border region has not only been in the grips of Governor Abbott over the last few years, but former President Donald Trump also made it a core priority as he promoted his cruel immigration policies. Trump visited the region a record five times between 2017 and 2019.[6] His hardline stance on immigration and his obsession with building a border wall gained him plenty of traction with his base in 2016.[7] And he's at it again, making a recent visit to Eagle Pass.[8]

Over the last year, Trump and Abbott's failed deterrence policies have been playing out in Eagle Pass every day. First, the state of Texas laid razor wire along the banks of the Rio Grande, then sent National Guard troops, buoys in the river followed, and now a complete occupation of Shelby Park. A once peaceful town with a shared binational fronterizo cultural fabric has become a battleground where local residents are disrupting false narratives, championing environmental and human rights, and celebrating their precious Rio Grande, which is a lifeline and a sanctuary for many.

A Call to Action

As a result of Abbott, Trump, and extremist Republican elected officials' political theater, armed extremist militias were inspired to descend on Eagle Pass in early February 2024 in support of Texas' cruel deterrence policies. The "Take Back Our Border" convoy wreaked havoc on the Eagle Pass community with several reported confrontations, threatening the safety of local residents.[9]

This prompted Presente.org, the Eagle Pass Border Coalition, and United We Dream to launch a campaign urging the U.S. Department of Justice (DOJ) to investigate the extremist militias who visited Eagle Pass and take decisive action to restore access to Shelby Park, a cherished public space community members have not been able to access since January 2024. Subsequently, 60 local, state, and national human and environmental rights organizations and thousands of activists joined us in sending a letter to the DOJ uplifting our requests.[10]

The letter states:

> Constituencies from across the country have joined our calls in defense of human and environmental rights and in asking the DOJ to act swiftly. Extremist groups are bursting at the seams and our communities are extremely concerned that more militias will descend on the U.S.-Mexico border and threaten our safety. We look forward to your leadership in taking swift action to ameliorate this injustice.

Amerika Garcia Grewal, a dedicated member of the Eagle Pass Border Coalition and Border Vigil, embodies the spirit of grassroots activism. "Hate and anti-immigrant sentiment have no place in our nation. We urgently need the DOJ's leadership. Investigate these extremists and get us our park and river back." Grewal's voice is one of hope, inspiring others to join the fight.

A Path Forward

We're in yet another pivotal emergency election year where Latine and migrant communities are confronting a deluge of hate, fear-mongering, and policies that are putting our ecosystems and human lives at risk. As our communities have done for decades, we've risen to the occasion by organizing for a more inclusive, equitable, and sustainable way of life. 2024 will require millions of us to take consistent action to truly reimagine and transform the culture and politics of our nation. And border communities in Texas are up for the challenge.

So, what does democracy truly look like? The promise of the United States is democracy – to directly participate in a system of government in which the people hold the ruling power. And Latine communities, more than 60 million strong, are poised to attain greater political power and shape the United States in ways that can turn that promise into reality, ushering in a bold new era of transformative change.

According to the Pew Research Center, the Latine electorate is rapidly expanding, with an estimated 36.2 million eligible voters in 2022, up from 32.3 million in 2020.[11] This represents a significant portion of the overall growth in eligible voters, highlighting the increasing influence of Latine voters in shaping the political landscape.

Moreover, the youthfulness of the Latine population further amplifies their potential impact. As the youngest demographic group in the United States, Latine voters represent an incredible force for change. Once their trust is earned, they emerge as steadfast supporters and advocates for their chosen causes, wielding considerable influence for decades to come.

Voter power, however, needs to be accompanied by more hands-on engagement and much greater investment with Latine voters. Drawing from the lessons of past electoral cycles, it is clear that strategic engagement is key to translating growing voter numbers into tangible political power.

Amidst the feverish attacks on our shared humanity, there exists incredible hope and a chance to unite with 60 million new Americans who are reshaping the very fabric of U.S. culture and democracy.

Notes

1 Emily Hernandez, "What is Operation Lone Star? Gov. Greg Abbott's Controversial Border Mission, Explained," *The Texas Tribune*, March 30, 2022, https://www.texastribune.org/2022/03/30/operation-lone-star-texas-explained/.
2 "US: Texas Officials Put Migrants in Danger," *Human Rights Watch*, July 20, 2023, https://www.hrw.org/news/2023/07/20/us-texas-officials-put-migrants-danger.
3 Acacia Coronado and Valerie Gonzalez, "Texas Prepares to Deploy Rio Grande Buoys in Governor's Latest Effort to Curb Border Crossings," *The Associated Press*, July 7, 2023, https://apnews.com/article/buoys-texas-immigration-rio-grande-mexico-522e45febd880de1453460370043a25f.
4 Zachary Mueller, "The Insurrection on January 6, the Great Replacement Theory, and the Ongoing Threat to Democracy," *America's Voice*, January 5, 2024, https://americasvoice.org/blog/the-insurrection-on-january-6-the-great-replacement-theory-and-the-ongoing-threat-to-democracy/.
5 Russell Contreras, "Anti-immigrant Rhetoric Sparks Fears of More Hate Crimes against Latinos," *Axios*, March 7, 2024, https://www.axios.com/2024/03/07/latinos-immigration-rhetoric-fears-hate-crimes.

6 Alexis Egeland, "Timeline: Donald Trump's Five Visits to the Border as President," *AZCentral*, April 5, 2019, https://www.azcentral.com/story/news/politics/2019/04/05/timeline-donald-trumps-five-visits-border-president/3377674002/.

7 Stephen Collinson and Jeremy Diamond, "Trump on Immigration: No Amnesty, no Pivot," *CNN*, September 1, 2016, https://www.cnn.com/2016/08/31/politics/donald-trump-immigration-speech/index.html.

8 R. Arelis Hernández, "Biden and Trump Visits to Texas Offer a Tale of Two Border Cities," *The Washington Post*, February 29, 2024, https://www.washingtonpost.com/nation/2024/02/29/biden-trump-texas-border-brownsville-eagle-pass/.

9 David Martin Davies, "Eagle Pass Residents on Edge as Texas Gov. vows to Expand Border Operations," *Texas Public Radio*, February 7, 2024, https://www.tpr.org/border-immigration/2024-02-07/right-wing-border-convoy-leaves-eagle-pass-residents-on-edge.

10 "Demanding Justice: Eagle Pass Residents Call for DOJ Investigation into Extremists Militias," *Presente.org*, March 15, 2024, https://presente.org/2024/03/demanding-justice-eagle-pass-residents-call-for-doj-investigation-into-extremist-militias/.

11 J. Krostad, J.S. Passel, A. Budiman, and A. Natarajan, "Key Facts about Hispanic Eligible Voters in 2024," January 10, 2024, https://www.pewresearch.org/short-reads/2024/01/10/key-facts-about-hispanic-eligible-voters-in-2024/.

13 Saving the Dead, Making the Future

Public History against Fascism

Mark Soderstrom

The battle over the future can be viewed equally as one over the past. In this conversation, public historian Mark Soderstrom addresses the unique challenges that the rise of the right poses for the national conversation.

Toppling False Idols

Editors: There is a sense that the right always has the upper hand when it comes to, if not history itself, if not the study of history, then when it comes to talking with the public. But that's something that we need to interrogate in the light of the current elections and as we try to understand whether there were any gains in the last few years – especially in terms of the institutional infrastructure as well as the legislative environment.

Mark Soderstrom: There's a lot here. Walter Benjamin once said something to the effect that, "Under fascism, even the dead are not safe."[1] And to me, that's the import of this election; some of how we shape our future is how we remember our past. Therefore, the right is very invested in rewriting and retaking the past. In some respects, recent historical gains have been very threatening to the right, which explains the viciousness of the backlash that we are seeing.

As a public historian and someone who teaches public history, I generally think in terms of how far we have to go. But we also need to appreciate how much progress we have made. Charles Meigs' statue is no longer in Harlem. Robert E. Lee no longer dominates Monument Avenue in Richmond. Teddy Roosevelt is not sitting astride his horse towering over an African and a Native man in front of the National History Museum in New York City, on one of the busiest avenues in the world.

The conversations around those statues are even more significant. They have led people to reconsider the past in ways that also make people reconsider their future. And it's not just an American phenomenon. Edward Colston no longer stands over the harbor in Bristol. Protesters threw his statue *into* the

DOI: 10.4324/9781003544371-15

harbor. There are matters that should still concern us, but there are also ways that we have made progress in the last few years, and we should not fail to recognize that.

Editors: Have those movements translated into a changing public conscious-
ness, or do they index some other forms of power, perhaps?
Soderstrom: I really think *both*. There is certainly the sort of power on the ground to make change: three of those statue removals are post George Floyd, and the power of those protests made those statues come down. But I think those events wouldn't have taken that shape without a lot of groundwork and conversation and historical work and consciousness shifting that happened before those events. So yes, both.

One example: In my home state of Minnesota, the flag and the seal have finally been changed after decades of Native protest. The flag had been the state seal on a blue background. It was drawn by Seth Eastman and depicts a white pioneer plowing a field with a musket and an ax leaning against a stump while a Native American in full feather headdress rides off into the sunset. And if that were not enough, Eastman's wife wrote a poem to go with it about how "'brave warrior,' it's time for you to give up the plains, the waters, the forests, they're the white man's now." And it's a terrible image of genocide that has flown over the statehouse of Minnesota for a century and a half. It has offended Native populations for most of that time, but addressing it has taken a lot of work to change the state's consciousness. And it also required changes in power. This didn't happen until the Democrats took the governor-ship and the state Senate and House. The flag has now changed, and the state seal now contains the Dakota name for the region and a loon instead of this image of genocide.

New Narratives in Old Houses

Editors: There is a certain ambivalence over changing the representations of
the past in that it feels as if we're closing the door on past domination but
without any substantive redistribution or actual coming to terms with the
past. So how do you approach this question?
Soderstrom: That's a difficult question; some people may want to just tear down statues and stop there. Obviously, that's not enough. One place where we could think about progress would be Monticello, Thomas Jefferson's home. Clint Smith has written eloquently in *How the Word Is Passed* about how history transmits knowledge, racial hierarchy, and oppression.[2] And he writes about visiting Monticello. One of the things that Monticello has done is to create a tour that focuses on the Hemings family[3] – Sally Hemings was Thomas Jefferson's mistress, mother to six of his children. This was a bitterly fought battle, taking years to prove

what the Hemings family knew to be true. She was also the daughter of Jefferson's father-in-law. Jefferson's slave, mistress, was also his wife's half-sister. I think the power there lies in a fundamental transformation of one of the hallmarks of the country. The people who run Monticello are now not just telling the victorious story of Jefferson, they're also telling a story about a woman who bore Jefferson's children, who was unable to fully give consent to sexual relations.

It is a very troubling story that gets at something hidden by the usual triumphal narrative. I think there is an actual change in terms of trying, as historians and public historians, to expand and clarify the narrative. My students in public history are exceptionally open and interested in thinking about trying to tell under-represented and ignored stories. I think, by and large, this is why many people are attracted to public history, and I think that's important work and work that must happen for the public to recognize where inequities in the present come from.

Fostering Communities

Editors: Certainly in universities, we've gained some progress in terms of challenging the past and also challenging the particular institution's past. As we step away from these public sites and universities and get more into communities, do you see history changing? Is there a public history infrastructure where the broader public can engage in these conversations?

Soderstrom: I was trained by fairly radical public historians who think about public history as a community project, as community work, as community organizing, and there is certainly a thread of that in the discipline. I try to encourage that in my students when they think about projects, and I think that's growing. One of my students did a wonderful project in an African-American neighborhood on teaching people how to think about preserving their own history, their own records and photographs. I think that we always need more of that, and I think in some respects, change is easier at that level. It is interesting to see that it has reached up into the more formal bureaucracies and institutions where change is also happening.

Inclusion Bottom to Top

Editors: So as we go forward, telling the story of redlining, telling the story of where people could get jobs and where they were basically cut off from jobs, where you see these smaller projects proceeding, should we have a federal government that is unfriendly to them? Do you see within certain

states the infrastructure to conduct better conversations and to protect
efforts like those of your students?

Soderstrom: I remain optimistic in that regard. People have done amazing historical work in harsh times. The Mapping Prejudice project in
Minneapolis started before 2016 and continued even with an ascendant
Trump and when there were significant Republican presences in state
government. Kirsten Delegard has done amazing work starting on her
own with records in a basement and has now garnered institutional support and created a community around the work.[4] She has a staff, she has
access to records, she has some tech support; but most importantly, she
has people from the community come in and work through Minneapolis's
deeds and documenting racial restrictions on home sales and home ownership. And it has become a model for other cities to consider in terms
of its community-organized nature. She's doing stunning work, and it is
starting to reshape urban policy in Minneapolis.

There are places and initiatives that can be moved forward at the local level,
the community level, the county level, and possibly in certain states. But the
kind of backlash that we see in places like Florida creates a chilling effect
that makes people and teachers police themselves because these laws are so
unclear. So, I also think history has been more effective with a strong federal
presence that's supportive.

In terms of thinking about protecting the dead, one of the federal initiatives
that I think has been underappreciated is the federal government's reinterpre-
tation of the Native American Graves Protection and Repatriation Act, with
new enforcement mechanisms.[5] It was passed 30 years ago, but there are still
hundreds of thousands of remains and looted sacred objects being held in
museums and institutions from the tribes. This is because initially the tribes
had to prove their right to those objects and those remains. Now, the Biden
administration has reversed that power, and it's dramatic. Tribes now have the
primary claim and *museums have to prove* why they can keep these objects.
The day after that changed, the Natural History Museum in New York City
had to close 10,000 square feet of Native galleries because after 30 years, their
objects were still not in compliance with the Act.

Thinking about the community work in places like Minnesota, many
museums didn't have to close their galleries because 11 recognized tribes
there have been working steadily for 30 years. The tribal organizations have
been working on getting the federal mandate enforced for decades. This is a
dramatic demonstration of what a supportive federal administration can do
that could not have happened at the state level or the county level. And I think
it's an underappreciated victory at the federal level.

Locally and at the state level, with institutions and individual historians that are serious about how to work with communities – not delivering

history to communities but assisting communities in developing their own history – there are grounds for hope. These projects are happening in small ways all around the country. For example, there is a labor history project in Washington state that has worked with local unions and the local community to create a local labor history project. It's a success story.[6]
Many projects are small, so they're easy to miss.

In the West Bank neighborhood in Minneapolis,[7] the West Bank history project worked very hard at finding ways to try to get people involved to write their own memories as the neighborhood was changing. "What was your experience here?" I have friends in the historic field who have very exciting projects reaching out through the internet to create gateways for people to take internet tours of their old neighborhoods and to write their own memories; that is, to place their own lives into the historical record, and in that respect to tie themselves to place and time and history and to other people who are contributing memories.

And in vibrant neighborhoods over generations, there are generations of difference. You can see your story from the 1950s, but you can see a Hmong immigrant story of the 1980s in the same place, and you're both talking about the same block. That, to me, is very hopeful, if we can develop those stories, because communities don't stay the same, they're not homogeneous. Those community stories embrace a kind of difference that I think is healthy and necessary. They are exciting and really where these things need to start because larger institutions are slower and will only follow.

Laboring History

Editors: In the last few years, we've seen something of a renaissance of the labor movement. Not only do we have more assertive organizing happening at, say, Amazon warehouses and even more difficult places to organize such as Starbucks, but the older unions like the UAW are out there in a much more militant form than in recent years. How do you see labor history entering the public history conversation in the present period?

Soderstrom: Well, that's a challenge. This is interesting because I think one of the strengths of public history is that it has always been interested in the history of daily life and working people, going back all the way to the first open-air museum opening in Stockholm in 1893, where they brought together normal people's residences, cottages, farmhouses, and tradesman's houses. That continues as a very strong theme. You go to any historic site; if there's a blacksmith shop there operating, it's probably the most visited area in a historic site. People are drawn to the histories of daily life. That said, labor history has its own set of challenges for public history, and there are a lot of public historians calling for more union and formal labor history, trying to find ways to do it.

It's a struggle: These things require resources, sites require interpretation and funding, and they require permissions at county, state, and federal levels. Many states and many politicians are unwilling to get involved in what is seen as potentially politically divisive. Chambers of commerce often don't like to fund exhibits about strikes that were against their own members. Therefore, trying to find ways to work with labor has been a challenge for public historians. Now, monuments have gone up at Ludlow,[8] monuments have gone up at the Battle of Deputies Run in Minneapolis.[9] We, of course, have wonderful examples where there's a powerful labor presence in the Lowell Historic District where the mills are preserved.[10] But it has been a struggle in the last decade to find ways to bring union history into public spaces. That's just more difficult.

We could look at Concord, New Hampshire. The state put up a fairly innocuous historical marker near the birthplace of Elizabeth Gurley Flynn, recognizing her as a labor organizer and feminist. They put it up on May 1, 2023, and Republican Governor Chris Sununu took it down on May 15, 2023.[11] I think this is an area where public historians have desire, but funding is a challenge. Unions need to think about their role in preserving their own past. In 2017, the United Mine Workers of America were able to restore a monument at the site of the Ludlow massacre, memorializing the victims of that struggle.[12] And monuments are victories! But they are steps. We need to find ways to reach more people with more dynamic community models of union public history. And while there are lots of people out there doing that work in small ways, I hope that unions are able to find ways to build on the work of entities like The Labor Heritage Foundation.[13] It's something I hope to see more of.

Attacking History

Editors: What do you think has conditioned right-wing responses like those of Sununu?

Soderstrom: Here's where Benjamin's observation that "Under fascism even the dead aren't safe" applies. Some on the right have been spooked by gains by centrists and the liberal left in the conversations around history. We've seen the backlash in the creation of a 1776 Project, specifically aimed at refuting Nikole Hannah-Jones's 1619 Project.[14] The 1776 Project initiation was held in the National Archives Building without inviting any of the national archivists, or any representatives of the American Historical Association or the Organization of American Historians. Basically, it was a publicity front for Trump. And we see the same happening around the country.

In Texas, there's been some talk about modifying and changing the Alamo, perhaps actually including some of the Tejano voices that were excluded, as well as some of the Mexican perspective, and correcting a little bit of the history. The Texas revolt was basically slaveholders revolting against a newly independent Mexico that had abolished slavery. The Texans were the slaveholders, and abolition in Mexico threw terror into the Texas Anglo establishment, resulting in their revolt. In recent times, we see the Texas Lieutenant Governor cancel a historic event at the Texas Historical Society with the authors of a monograph, *Forget the Alamo*,[15] the morning before it happens. The Governor then creates the 1836 Project – again, specifically targeting the 1619 Project, and specifically to challenge the history that every historian knows about the Texas Revolt. The power of that backlash, I think, comes because the right does not feel in control of the historical conversation and the communities of history that are out there at the moment.

The Second Time as Farce

Editors: If our task is about protecting the dead, perhaps even vindicating their lives and their stories, how does this play out with respect to the public conversation on immigration? And what do you think a future federal government run by the right would see as its agenda in the coming four years?

Soderstrom: Well, Trump is interesting. Trump is obsessed with history! Famously, Trump's Lowes Island golf course, on the Potomac,[16] erected a Civil War monument there – to where "the Union and southern troops met at this river crossing. The battle was so fierce that it became known as the River of Blood." The only problem is that the battle *never* happened. It's completely made up. And when historians have said, "No, there was never a battle here," Trump actually says, "How would you know? Were you there?"[17] He's contemptuous of history and basic truth.

Trump is invested in a kind of patriotic white supremacism that reaches back to the Gilded Age, before the Progressive Era. The kind of order that they want to go back to makes history a weapon, one that they are willing to fabricate entirely. They don't need records; they don't need an event to have happened. They just need to create a useful story to use. And I think that that golf course monument tells us what we would look forward to – it is a crass historical narrative that bears no relationship to what historians have worked so hard to try to discover, think about, and carefully craft as stories of our United States.

Notes

1   "In every era the attempt must be made anew to wrest tradition away from a conformism that is about to overpower it. The Messiah comes not only as the redeemer, he comes as the subduer of Antichrist. Only that historian will have the gift of fanning the spark of hope in the past who is firmly convinced that even the dead will

not be safe from the enemy if he wins. And this enemy has not ceased to be victorious." Walter Benjamin, "On the Concept of History" (1940) in *Selected Writings. Volume 4: 1938 – 1940.* Ed. by Howard Eiland and Michael W. Jennings, 1st pbk. ed (Cambridge, MA: Belknap Press of Harvard University Press, 2006), p. 391.

2 Clint Smith, *How the Word Is Passed: A Reckoning with the History of Slavery across America,* 1st edition (New York, Boston, and London: Little, Brown and Company, 2021).

3 "From Slavery to Freedom Tour," Monticello, accessed April 2, 2024, https://www.monticello.org/visit/tickets-tours/from-slavery-to-freedom/.

4 "Kirsten Delegard | Mapping Prejudice," accessed April 2, 2024, https://mapping-prejudice.umn.edu/about-us/team/kirsten-delegard.

5 "Interior Department Takes Next Steps to Update Native American Graves Protection and Repatriation Act | U.S. Department of the Interior," *Press Release,* October 13, 2022, https://www.doi.gov/pressreleases/interior-department-takes-next-steps-update-native-american-graves-protection-and-1.

Logan Jaffe and Mary Hudetz, "The American Museum of Natural History to Close Exhibits Displaying Native American Belongings," *ProPublica,* January 26, 2024, https://www.propublica.org/article/american-museum-natural-history-to-close-native-american-exhibits.

6 Governor Inslee agrees with this assessment, see Jay Inslee, "Washington Is a Leading State for Workers – a Long History of State Action Paved the Way," *Washington State Governor's Office* (blog), September 2, 2022, https://medium.com/wagovernor/washington-is-a-leading-state-for-workers-a-long-history-of-state-action-paved-the-way-496305bc6c3e.

7 To learn more about the locale's history, see Ellie Malmon-Andrews et al., "Tracing Displacement and Disinvestment on UMN's West Bank," *ArcGIS StoryMaps,* March 22, 2022, https://storymaps.arcgis.com/stories/032df86fecc14421a5297f718ceb5f1f.

8 Shanna Lewis, "Preservation Work at the Ludlow Massacre Site Revealed Hidden Symbols. They'll Never Be Seen Again," *Colorado Public Radio,* November 18, 2021, https://www.cpr.org/2021/11/18/ludlow-massacre-site-preservation-work/.

9 Ehsan Alam, "The Minneapolis Teamsters' Strike of 1934," *MinnPost,* May 8, 2023, http://www.minnpost.com/mnopedia/2023/05/the-minneapolis-teamsters-strike-of-1934/.

10 "Lowell National Historical Park (U.S. National Park Service)," accessed April 2, 2024, https://www.nps.gov/lowe/index.htm.

11 "Judge to Decide Whether Gurley Flynn Historic Marker Lawsuit Will Move Forward," *New Hampshire Public Radio,* January 25, 2024, https://www.nhpr.org/nh-news/2024-01-25/judge-hears-arguments-on-whether-gurley-flynn-historic-marker-case-will-move-forward.

12 Project Update: Ludlow Tent Colony Massacre Site, accessed April 4, 2024, https://coloradopreservation.org/project-update-ludlow-tent-colony-massacre-site-cellar-restoration/.

13 Home - Labor Heritage Foundation, accessed April 4, 2024, https://www.laborheritage.org/content.aspx?page_id=0&club_id=533040.

14 Gillian Brockell, "'A Hack Job,' 'Outright Lies': Trump Commission's '1776 Report' Outrages Historians," *Washington Post,* January 22, 2021, https://www.washingtonpost.com/history/2021/01/19/1776-report-historians-trump/.

Adam Serwer, "The Fight Over the 1619 Project Is Not About the Facts," *The Atlantic* (blog), December 23, 2019, https://www.theatlantic.com/ideas/archive/2019/12/historians-clash-1619-project/604093/.

15 Bryan Burrough, Chris Tomlinson, and Jason Stanford, *Forget the Alamo: The Rise and Fall of an American Myth* (New York: Penguin Press, 2021).

16 "About Our Courses," accessed April 2, 2024, https://www.trumpnationaldc.com/golf.

17 Joyce Chen, "Trump's Golf Course Plaque Honors Fake Civil War Battle," *Rolling Stone*, August 17, 2017, https://www.rollingstone.com/politics/politics-news/donald-trumps-golf-course-plaque-honors-fake-civil-war-battle-253119/.

Intermission (Take Action!)

14 Values, Villain, Vision

Messaging to Mobilize Our Base and Persuade the Conflicted

Anat Shenker-Osorio

Introduction: Say What You're For and Call Out the Opposition

If we want to "heal our divided society" and "make good the promises of American democracy to all citizens," we must instill in people a desire to take and sustain action for progressive policies and candidates.

Over a decade of evidence garnered through surveys, randomized-controlled trials, field experiments, and, more importantly, real-world campaigns for progressive issues and candidates have brought to light a set of consistent messaging principles for *mobisuasion*. In other words, mobilizing our base and persuading the conflicted for our causes and candidates.

The first among these is *Say What You're For*. All too often, progressive messaging relies upon negation, from "immigrants are not taking our jobs" to "we do not have voter fraud" to "tackling climate change will not harm our economy." Much like Nixon declaring "I am not a crook" made viewers suspect him of criminality, negations lend airtime and therefore credence to what we're attempting to refute. In addition, we tend to offer negative demands such as stopping voter suppression, ending mass incarceration, banning fracking, and so on. These fail to paint the "beautiful tomorrow" – offering people a sense of what the world would be like were our policies to be put into practice.

And at the same time, we must convey a critical contrast between our proposition and the opposition, clearly indicating what's on the line if those who seek to silence voices, restrict votes, and pervert values gain power.

Right now, our most common explanations for inequities – *gap between rich and poor*, *health disparities*, "Black people were admitted to jail at more than four times the rate of White people," and so on, simply describe how outcomes differ between groups. This is all *what* and no *why*. These formulations leave it up to the audience to fill in the cause. But instead of accurately seeing structural forces at play, people all too readily blame individuals for their plight and are moved against progressive solutions. For example, whites hearing about racial disparities in deaths from COVID-19 were more likely to believe the government was doing too much for pandemic relief. And

DOI: 10.4324/9781003544371-17

when penal institutions were presented as having more Black inmates, white respondents favored more punitive measures.

In short, when we fail to make clear that a problem is person-made, it becomes challenging or even impossible to demand it be person-fixed. When we fail to correctly identify who is responsible, we risk feeding the all-too-ready assumptions that people experiencing poor outcomes are the ones responsible for this.

For the purposes of promoting the Kerner Commission's aims, we must make clear to our audiences how our present-day divisions emerged, identify who is deliberately blocking effective solutions, and unpack how they're able to thwart what continue to be majoritarian preferences. In short, we cannot create public will for a fairer, freer, more just America unless we correctly identify what impedes that will.

The very idea that our society "is divided" suggests this arose from the ether. That we are somehow drifting apart like continents breaking away from what was once Pangea. Further, this gives credence to the troubling idea that "both sides" are equally responsible. That asking people to respect pronouns or rein in police violence is somehow akin to seizing the basic rights and freedoms of targeted groups.

In fact, stoking and exacerbating divisions is a political strategy authoritarian leaders pursue in order to claim and hold onto power. While the selected scapegoats differ and the phrases used to shame and blame them come in many forms, all authoritarian leaders know that the quickest route to an "us" is railing against a "them," a vital precursor to obfuscating plans to destroy democracy and rule only for the already wealthy and most powerful few.

We see this in Orbán's Hungary, where Roma people are vilified and denied justice. We saw it in the main slogan of the Brexit campaign, which vowed to "take back control" over immigration. And we watched Brazil's Bolsonaro rail against "gender ideology" and lambast LGBTQ to seize power. It's no surprise that an ever-present authoritarian faction in America has continued to carry the Tiki Torch to advance what once justified the enslavement of people from Africa and Native genocide, which became Jim Crow, Nixon's Southern Strategy, the Tea Party, and now the MAGA Movement.

Fortunately, we have hope-inducing examples to follow of not merely overcoming the politics of cruelty, but of making the absolute most of a very narrow governing majority and implementing policies to shore up democracy, address inequality, and improve life for people of all races, backgrounds, and genders. Arguably, the most comprehensive domestic example of this comes from Minnesota.

The "Minnesota Miracle": Rebuffing Right-Wing Race Baiting to Achieve Progressive Governance

In 2016, Donald Trump came within roughly 40,000 votes of winning Minnesota – the best a Republican had done at the top of the ticket in this state since Ronald Reagan in 1984. Minnesota Republicans saw in this landmark performance an opportunity to amass greater power utilizing the time-honored right-wing populist strategy: divide in order to conquer.

A largely white state with a recognizable Somali-American population, thanks to the immigrants who first settled there before the 1980s, joined by refugees fleeing civil war in the early 1990s, Minnesota seemed fertile terrain for nurturing the Republican seeds of anti-Black race-baiting, anti-refugee xenophobia, and anti-Muslim fear-mongering. On cue, state Republicans, who seized control of the state senate and held the house in 2016, accelerated attacks on Somali-run daycare centers, accusing them of funneling funds intended to subsidize childcare into suitcases full of cash sent to Africa to finance terrorism. Right-wing media in the state had their typical field day spreading these stories, stoking and exacerbating fear of this "other" in order to increase their political power by promising to protect "real Minnesotans" from this threat.

This tried-and-true dog whistle strategy, using racially coded invectives to evoke and provoke grievances among whites against people of color, had proved integral to Trump's success in the state and beyond it. Indeed, Trump unofficially entered the political arena by sowing doubts about President Obama's origins and faith. And Trump doubled down on this when he officially launched his bid for the presidency, riding his golden elevator into the bowels of xenophobia against Mexican Americans, with talk of "illegals" and promises of a border wall. In this, Trump dialed up the volume on standard Republican phrases like "welfare queens" and "inner city crime," language that conveys that Black and brown people cause harm to "hardworking Americans" (read: white people) without actually ever naming racial categories.

Yet, 2016 was the election where pundits penned seemingly endless op-eds attributing Hillary Clinton's loss to her having spoken too openly and frequently about race. Perhaps most famously, Mark Lilla penned the piece that would become its own genre – finger-wagging about the limitations and dangers of what was once called "political correctness," renamed "identity politics," and now recast as "cultural issues" or "wokeness."

Both nationally and in Minnesota, this argument played out not merely in the media but became the very heart of hand-wringing over how to regroup and reorient after seeing the Midwestern "Blue Wall" crumble. The diagnosis offered was that "working class voters," who, to hear pundits tell it, aren't just white but generally male, were turning against the Democratic Party and progressive policies. The standard advice – an echo of similar guidance called "triangulation" in Bill Clinton's era and "Popularism" today – was to moderate our message, silence any talk of purportedly polarizing issues like race and policing, immigrant rights and abortion, and stick to universally beloved economic promises.

To be sure, the advice that engendering support for progressive policies and politicians requires championing only poll-tested issues like lowering prices and creating jobs seems logical. Why wouldn't you say only the things that nearly everyone likes and no one outright hates? However, this approach continuously fails in practice because it ignores the realities of how people come to judgments, what is required to change their minds, and what inspires them to take and sustain necessary actions to achieve policy victories.

Not talking about race is great advice, unless your issue is race. And when you're attempting to "reverse the exploitation of Americans by the privileged and the rigged system" and "expose and advocate against the denial of exploitation," it is. Second, in reality, there are no race-neutral issues. While one could argue for things like more funding for public education, securing voting rights, or providing affordable housing without naming race, opponents of these endeavors will always bring race into the picture.

Indeed, as Ian Haney López has laid out, the true purpose of the dog whistle politics strategy is to impugn people of color in order to undermine belief in government itself. The precise evidence-based policies that the Kerner Commission championed are portrayed as wasteful government "handouts" to the "undeserving," tacitly coded as people of color, unfairly seized from "hardworking taxpayers," whom we're meant to understand as white. Opponents of these measures convince voters that we cannot have universal benefits like labor protections, free public education through university, or single-payer healthcare because there is no "us." Instead, there is a "them," who do not merit any public benefits.

Fortunately for Minnesota, decades of organizing and robust multi-racial coalition building left them clear-eyed and ready to effectively address the racially divisive messaging that Republicans had long been pumping out.

During the 2016 campaign, organizers knocking on doors in rural Minnesota documented a repeated pattern. When they would show up touting progressive economic policies – from creating quality jobs to making childcare more affordable – voters would register approval. But their enthusiasm would falter as they trot out right-wing talking points about immigrants coming for those employment opportunities or stealing those childcare funds. In short, economic promises – desirable as they were – could not withstand the right-wing storyline blaming immigrants, and Somalis more specifically, for the troubles of "real Minnesotans."

Rather than fall into despair, state leaders from Faith in Minnesota, Education Minnesota, SEIU Minnesota, and Our Minnesota Future joined in on a national project taking shape that would become what we now call the Race Class Narrative (RCN).

In 2018, this research project began thanks to the efforts of *Dog Whistle Politics* and *Merge Left* author Ian Haney López, who approached me to help craft and test messaging to settle the tiresome debate about whether to speak exclusively of racial issues or center our political appeals in race-neutral class rhetoric. Haney López and I teamed up with Heather McGhee, at that time the president of Demos, and began qualitative and quantitative exploration with Lake Research Partners and Brilliant Corners nationally and within California, Indiana, Ohio, and, of course, Minnesota. In this, we worked alongside SEIU's Racial Justice Center with communications director Tinselyn Simms. Anika Fassia steered this whole process – from research design to dissemination of findings.

Over the course of 10 focus groups and five surveys, we found that messaging fusing together race and class didn't merely best standard opposition rhetoric. It out-performed status quo left-wing approaches that eschew mention of race among voters across racial groups. Minnesota took this even further, conducting an 800-person canvassing field experiment. Voters were shown a real Republican flier replete with racially-coded invectives and then one of two rebuttals: one was race neutral and the other utilized the newly crafted RCN approach.

Among white respondents, a majority agreed with the initial dog whistle script. When these respondents were shown the class-only progressive flyer and asked which candidate they would select, 55% stuck with the racially divisive politician, and 44% shifted to the progressive candidate. But for those shown the race-class message the numbers flipped. Only 43% stayed with the conservative candidate while 57% switched to the progressive who addressed race and class together.

In 2020 retesting, we validated these previous findings and found RCN more effective with voters of color and white voters than race-only storylines that argue for equality and justice without addressing class-based economic inequities. The same held true for various experiments run independently by pollsters and academics, as well as our own further testing.

RCN moved those with mixed feelings on questions of racial justice, economic policymaking, and the role of government toward more progressive views across the board. At the same time, among respondents in agreement with us on the broad spectrum of progressive values and policies, it increased their desire to take action and abated their cynicism, helping them believe that we could come together to make the improvements in our society that the Kerner Commission championed.

This engage the base and persuade the middle approach is integral to RCN. Our strategy rests upon the belief that turnout *is* persuasion because if your base won't carry the message, the middle will not hear it. Our efforts to create a better world do not enjoy the luxury of endless advertising budgets.

We must have our choir singing from the same songbook in order to ensure that the congregation hears the joyful noise and goes out to convert new adherents.

RCN uses a tried-and-tested messaging architecture. We shorthand this as *Values Villain Vision*. It begins not with a recitation of the many problems we confront, but rather an evocation of a shared value with an explicit mention of race or whatever dimension of division the opposition is bringing to the fore. This shared value is our opening *say what we're for* salvo.

The value named is selected on the basis of the issue to be discussed and explicitly names race, class, gender, geography, and/or faith – depending on the axes of division the opposition is promoting. For example, in a campaign to raise wages, we could say, "No matter what we look like or what's in our wallets, most of us believe that people who work for a living ought to earn a living." An effort to promote universal single-payer care would kick off with "whether we're Black or white, Latino or Asian, Native or newcomer, if someone we love is ill or injured we want them to have the very best care without going bankrupt to get it." And a campaign to dismantle state restrictions on voting would begin "across race and places, in America, we believe that voters pick our leaders, our leaders do not pick their voters."

In fact, the original Kerner Commission report employed this RCN-style opening, saying, "it was time to make good the promises of American democracy to all citizens – urban and rural, white and black, Spanish-surname, American Indian and every minority group."

After we name a value relevant to the task at hand and insist it is shared across races, places of origin, zip codes, and/or genders, we move to articulating the problem we're confronting and do so naming the perpetrators who created it.

As mentioned earlier, the first step to solving any problem is recognizing its origins. Unfortunately, the nearly ubiquitous unsourced problem statements we tend to write, like "voting rights are under attack," "democracy is eroding," or "our Nation is moving toward two societies, one black, one white – separate and unequal," eclipse from view the actors behind these outcomes. Attacks on the franchise aren't of origins unknown. Our nation is not a fertilized egg dividing. People do things, and when these things harm other people, it is absolutely critical we make clear the culprits behind these misdeeds.

Thus, in RCN messaging, we call out these culprits in the *Villain* sentence after our opening *Value*. Returning to the example offered on raising wages, this second sentence could read as follows:

> But today, a handful of corporations and the politicians they pay for are holding down wages, while they point the finger at Black people, new immigrants, or people struggling to make ends meet, so we'll look the other way while they hoard profits from the wealth our work creates.

In addition to making clear there's a *who* behind our struggles, an effective *Villain* call-out does two other things. First, it exposes the right's strategy of deliberate division and scapegoating: it narrates the dog whistle, making visible and thus less effective how opponents of equality obfuscate their aims by blaming others for the harms they wreak upon us. If they can convince you that José, standing in front of Home Depot soliciting day labor, powerless to set public policy, is "taking your job," you'll fail to notice that Jeff Bezos actually did this deed. If they can recast their efforts to restrict voting under the guise of "election security" by inventing false claims about fraud, we will look the other way while Black folks in urban centers are made to stand in line for hours to exercise their most fundamental freedoms.

And, second, the *Villain* sentence tells us not just what the bad guys are up to but why they engage in their nefarious aims. Above, their motivation was listed as "hoard profits." A *Villain* sentence for a healthcare message would also indicate not only what opponents are doing but underscore the desires behind it. For illustration:

> But a wealthy and powerful few divide us based on what we look like, where we come from or who we love so they can keep refusing to pay what they owe in taxes to ensure all of us have the care our families need.

While the two examples offered here provide a profit-seeking backstory, as is fitting for the respective issues they address, an equally effective explanation is the pursuit of power by unscrupulous politicians. Especially when we're advocating for realizing our democracy or confronting injustices in things like policing and immigration policy, the more accurate way to convey what the right is up to is to describe their quest to seize or maintain control. Thus, in a message for voting rights, this second sentence would say,

> but today MAGA Republicans want to claim and hold power by taking away people's freedoms to pick our own leaders based on what we look like or where we live. They know that they cannot win by courting more voters and so they attempt to keep us from voting.

Finally, an RCN message ends by addressing what we most often see as our core obstacle to moving audiences to action. As public polling and ballot initiatives often prove, our opposition is not the opposition itself, but rather cynicism. It's not that people do not believe our ideas are right, but rather that they are not possible. Most Americans want more affordable healthcare, better wages and working conditions, equitable voting, quality schools for all, common-sense gun reforms, clean air and water, and so on. But since they feel these aims are unlikely to come to fruition, why bother giving up absolutely precious time and energy to lost causes?

This final *Vision* sentence paints the aforementioned "beautiful tomorrow." In this, we strive to *sell the brownie and not the recipe*; meaning that we do not expect the name of our policy to entice people but rather we lure them by narrating the outcomes the policy will deliver. Thus, for example, "paid family leave" becomes "you're there the first time your newborn smiles," and "voting rights" turns into "you decide who governs in your name" or "you have a hand in the rules that determine your future."

A concluding *Vision* sentence for raising wages would say, "by joining together we can rewrite the rules so all of us can earn a good living and live a good life." And for voting, it could say, "by demanding our leaders pass the Freedom to Vote Act, we can make this a place where 'we the people' includes all of us, no exceptions."

RCN works for both issue-specific messages, as we've just explored, and also to craft an overarching narrative. Coming back to Minnesota, we found that a particularly resonant opening value was group harmony and the vision centered on the Golden Rule:

> Minnesota's strength comes from our ability to be there for each other – to knit together people from different places and of different races into a community. For this to be a place of freedom for all, we cannot let a greedy few and the politicians they fund divide us based on what someone looks like, where they come from or how much money they have. It's time we talk to each other and stand up for anyone getting bullied or shut out by ugly rhetoric. We must pick leaders who honor the Golden Rule, treating others as they want to be treated. Together, we can make Minnesota a place where freedom and community are for everyone, no exceptions.

A full narrative, no matter how well-crafted, does not a winning campaign make. This is why, from its inception, RCN has operated on what we call a Three-Legged Stool model to build public will for causes and candidates. Leg one is building the choir: that is, getting disparate groups from across a state or issue area to agree to repeat the same message. It cannot be repeated enough how critical repetition is. Messages that are more familiar to audiences are routinely rated as more credible, convincing, and positive. This is because hearing something we already know creates cognitive ease – our brains are able to predict what comes next without effort. This, again, is why we focus so much on animating our "choir."

The second leg is writing the songbook. In essence, it involves undertaking research to arrive at a winning message – of the variety shared above – that will move conflicted voters and engage the base, ideally inspiring them to want to repeat our message.

Finally, we have the mounting of the multi-media production leg – that is creating digital ads, memes, events, radio announcements, collateral materials, visible swag, and so on to put the messaging in people's faces over and again.

Thus, once we completed the original RCN research, we created a branded campaign for the 2018 election called *Greater Than Fear*, with the tagline "in Minnesota we're better off together." The name was an intentional nod to "Greater Minnesota," the phrase used to name the rural parts of the state. This was the locus of the opposition's efforts to stir up fear, and so we directed our overarching brand straight at it. The tagline was an affirmative callback to Senator Paul Wellstone's saying, "we all do better when we all do better," which we were surprised to hear focus group respondents in the state offer up routinely.

We created a Greater Than Fear messaging guide for use by all the organizations in the coalition. This means we had a message repeating the branding to argue for driver's licenses for undocumented immigrants, one for increasing funding to public schools, another advocating for wage hikes, and yet another pushing back against anti-Muslim invectives. We trained thousands of organizers in this messaging and had them do their electoral canvassing in Greater Than Fear shirts.

We made digital and radio ads, full-color posters, bus ads, and printed materials. When Trump came to Rochester, Minnesota, we held a Greater Than Fear rally in lieu of an anti-Trump march, which would have simply given him more airtime. We created a "Dogs Against Dog Whistling" social media avatar that folks used to clap back at right-wing race-baiting and a dog-related GOTV event. During the Republican debate, we provided a "dog whistle" BINGO card to inoculate folks against their standard invectives by showing we could predict beforehand precisely what they'd say. In short, we found ways to amplify this branding and messaging in every way that we could.

In 2018, progressives swept the executive races – including a very tense Attorney General race for Black Muslim Democrat Keith Ellison – flipped the Minnesota House and won two U.S. Senate seats (there was a special election to fill Al Franken's vacated spot).

This same mighty coalition kept meeting weekly to decide which messages to amplify in between elections. Then, over the pandemic summer of 2020, George Floyd was murdered by Minneapolis police, and Republican Minnesota Senate Majority Leader Paul Gazelka asked, "where's the apology to the moms out in the suburbs scared to death about what's happening all around them, and seeing the glowing fire in Minneapolis-St. Paul?"

Greater Than Fear no longer seemed an apt sentiment given how real and understandable fear was among Black Minnesotans. Thus, while organizers kept using the RCN messaging framework, they selected *We Make Minnesota* as the 2020 overarching brand. They also developed a public safety message called Fund Our Lives.

In response to Gazelka's obvious attempts to pit "suburban moms" against people of color demanding justice within the Twin Cities, Faith in Minnesota developed an "I am a suburban mom" campaign wherein women of all races recorded videos declaring their desire for real safety, an end to police violence, and challenging perceptions of who really lives in the suburbs and what they believe. As ever, using an RCN framework to declare what we are for and push back against opposition efforts to divide, scapegoat, and sow fear.

Despite the enormous strain of COVID, the horrific distress of police brutality, and the challenges of the mass reckoning for racial justice birthed in Minnesota in 2020, progressives once again prevailed in the election.

These seasoned campaigners delivered again in 2022, finally achieving a Democratic trifecta by flipping the Minnesota House despite the predictions of a "Red Wave." Once again, Keith Ellison faced a challenging Attorney General race, given not merely his race and faith but his key role in bringing Derek Chauvin to trial and achieving an extraordinarily rare conviction against a police officer. Right-wing operatives threw every standard "law and order" trope at this race and still did not prevail because campaigners in Minnesota have mastered how to put forward an affirmative values-based narrative that calls out the other side for their politics of cruelty and entices a multi-racial coalition to come together for better.

With a one-seat majority, between January and May of 2023, Democrats passed 15 pieces of progressive legislation, including protecting abortion rights, providing free school meals, legalizing driver's licenses for undocumented people, increasing transit funding, codifying voting rights, and granting paid family and medical leave. These lawmakers were able to pass this astonishing sweep of laws – despite their narrow margin in government – because they had campaigned explicitly on a platform of racial and economic justice. They did not come into office offering a Republican-lite version of leadership. Voters chose them expecting to have progressive policy outcomes.

Minnesota may be the most comprehensive example of adopting effective messaging and truly implementing it. But it's far from the only one. Wisconsin, Michigan, and Pennsylvania also participated in RCN research and implementation, developing their own multi-racial coalitions to carry out effective messaging and help flip these states in 2020 and retain Democratic control in 2022. Indeed, the track record of wins, from school board races to Senate campaigns, spans across the country and even to the UK and Australia.

Concluding Thoughts: If You Want People to Come to Your Cause, Be Attractive

As Toni Cade Bambara said, "the role of the artist is to make the revolution irresistible." So too, I would argue, is the role of the activist. We must convey how the policies we seek to implement will make people's families, communities, and futures truly desirable. If we want people to come to our cause, we must *be attractive* – that is, provide a compelling vision that draws them in.

And, at the same time, we cannot forget that politics – and any efforts to change public policy absolutely require entangling ourselves in politics – isn't a game of solitaire. Our audiences do not hear only from us. They are subjected to the unending race-baiting and fear-mongering of our opposition. Thus, what we tell people must provide a clear origin story for present-day problems they know all too well and rebuff, or ideally inoculate against, the opposition's tale of who is to blame.

Finally, we must keep in mind that a message that no one hears is, by definition, not persuasive. A message is like a baton that must be passed from person to person. Thus, when we're often admonished that we're simply "preaching to the choir," the choir is where the good trouble, to use John Lewis's phrase, starts. And without them singing in harmony, we cannot move the congregation to convert new participants to our cause.

This essay is a lightly edited revision of a chapter that will appear in Curtis, A., Ed. (2025). Creating Justice in a Multiracial Democracy: New Will For Evidence-Based Policies That Work. New York: Teachers College Press.

15 Letter to College Students

Mia McLaughlin, Erin Miller, and
Kyoungnak Minn

Another day. You wake up, reach for your phone, and you are bombarded with videos and articles – another bombing, another school shooting, another day. We are oversaturated with media made up of various themes, but media that is implicitly political has impacted the motivations of our generation more than any generations that came before. As members of Gen Z, we were born into a chaotic world that has been deeply disturbed by the aftermath of 9/11, the 2008 recession, and a global pandemic. These events have left us with feelings of hopelessness in all forms: political, economic, and social. These feelings are then constantly reinforced by the media we consume daily, leading to one of the *biggest* and *most* educated generations feeling more powerless than the ones that came before. How can a single vote in an electoral college system make a difference in who becomes President? Who do we choose between a President that has threatened democracy like no other and a Presidential Administration that is complicit with the international horrors we are watching unfold at this very moment? How can my voice, my vote, my generation, do anything to affect the destruction and despair I see on my phone every day?

Every day it seems like we are drowning in another crisis our political elders are blissfully unaffected by, and outlining some of the crises we face is important to know what is at stake at the ballot. From the conception of our country, systemic and socialized racism has been an aggregate to our nation's well-being. On paper, racism seems to be solved due to "equal rights" such as voting. Yet, our generation is experiencing a new frontier of racism which is deeply systemic. Our POC communities are desperate to know how to survive and potentially thrive in a country that consistently creates barriers for them. How do you live in a country that was built on the hopes of immigrants but consistently denies those wishes for millions of families? In a country where you know that the police force meant to protect you is more likely to brutalize or kill you? Persistent racial inequality has been exacerbated and underscored by incidents such as the murder of George Floyd, the alarming rise of AAPI hate crimes, and the ongoing humanitarian disaster at the southern border, demanding urgent attention. This violence towards minority groups has only

DOI: 10.4324/9781003544371-18

increased with unregulated access to firearms across the states. Our "foundational" 2nd Amendment right has done nothing but create more division and more death in the United States. With school shootings and gun-related deaths skyrocketing, Republicans continue to offer "thoughts and prayers" while more young people are placed in the line of fire.

We have witnessed the continued assault on reproductive rights across the country. Since the fall of Roe, young women, particularly those of the BIPOC community, face a future that guarantees them fewer reproductive rights than their mothers and grandmothers before them. Republicans are keen to double down on dismantling access to birth control, further accelerating the GOP's assault on young women's fundamental human rights, despite the near-universal agreement on common-sense reproductive freedoms, such as in cases of rape, incest, or danger to the health of the mother.

Our generation has also become all too familiar with the worsening effects of economic inequality. Many of us struggle to imagine a future where we can become homeowners, overcome skyrocketing student loan debt, maintain access to affordable healthcare, and have enough financial stability to start our own families. Similarly, our generation is set to be the most impacted by climate change, as we bear witness every year to the spate of extreme weather events and natural disasters that are shrugged off as just a part of life. All of this is compounded by the mental health crisis our generation experiences, partially as a result of all this political uncertainty.

The elephant in the room is the horror of what is going on in Gaza. We have seen it all. Twitter, Instagram, and TikTok have exposed us to the bombing of hospitals and schools, the destruction of property, and the murder of innocents. Biden and his Democratic coalition most importantly, Kamala Harris - should not endorse the military-industrial complex that is pouring 14.3 billion dollars of taxpayer money to fuel the mass killings of so many innocent civilians. Yet, the US has continued to reject or abstain on numerous UN Security Council resolutions to call for a ceasefire. Persistently supporting Netanyahu and his far-right policies is not something that we wish for. This is an issue that is strongly felt by every American, not just those of our generation.

Biden's inaction in many of these areas is reprehensible'; we hope Harris will end US militarism. But we have to acknowledge how another Trump term would see our interests kicked to the curb and democratic norms decimated. To recap, Trump has turned his racist rhetoric into action. His termination of the DACA program and family separation policy at the southern border further endanger the lives of immigrant youth. His racist rhetoric also targeted the AAPI community in labeling the coronavirus the "China virus," increasing the number of hate crimes perpetrated against this community in recent years. His affiliation with white supremacist organizations like the Proud Boys is ongoing and can be summed up by his comments on Charlottesville's Unite the Right Rally when he infamously noted there were "very fine people on both sides." This point can be further driven home by pointing to the insurrection as a glaring example of his dominion over right-wing, white supremacist hate groups.

His appointment of Justice Kavanaugh, Justice Gorsuch, and Justice Coney Barrett was the nail in the coffin that sealed the fate of Roe v. Wade, marking a horrific loss for women's rights and impacting marginalized communities extensively. Even within the past year, Trump has championed on the campaign trail a potential abortion ban past 16 weeks and has spoken with his advisors about preventing the FDA from distributing critical reproductive healthcare drugs.

During his time in office, his administration saw the rollback of environmental protections like the weakening of emissions regulations, making it easier for big corporations to pollute our protected green spaces. Not only did he disregard our very vocal concerns about the urgency needed to tackle the changing climate, but Trump also eagerly raced to withdraw the United States from the Paris Climate Agreement. Furthermore, at his direction, his administration unleashed a spate of tax cuts for the wealthiest Americans, all while attempting to undermine the Affordable Care Act, jeopardizing our access to affordable healthcare. Trump has made it abundantly clear he intends to strip back our affordable access to healthcare by proposing cuts to Medicaid funding and weakening protections for pre-existing conditions. In the same vein, he specifically targeted the mental health services Medicaid covers and encouraged stigmatizing rhetoric, further isolating vulnerable groups. Furthermore, Trump gleefully proclaimed plans to ax the Public Service Loan Forgiveness program and cut funding for Pell Grants, which are critical in helping members of our generation afford college.

In terms of his foreign policy, members of Trump's circle have extensively made their views clear on the Palestinian people, as his son-in-law, Jared Kushner, spoke excitedly about plans to turn the Gaza Strip into a real estate opportunity. Trump himself indicated that individuals who don't vote for him are inherently antisemitic, further illustrating the disparity between his outdated, racist playbook and the progressive policies and values our generation holds dear. In short, Trump is a full-fledged, wholesale disaster who would trade our democratic rights away for a chance at power.

However, while these issues are monumental, the biggest concern all young voters should be aware of and actively fight against is the impending rollout of Project 2025. Trump, alongside his committee of cronies in Congress and several far-right think tanks, launched Project 2025 as a post-re-election agenda to promote the creation of a fascist, right-wing regime. The plans laid out within detail how Trump would go about stripping away the democratic rights of citizens, such as the right to free speech and democratic participation. While this may sound like every far-right extremist's wildest dream come true, this project is becoming increasingly more realistic and tangible, with concrete policy proposals already set to be rolled out on day one of a second Trump term. Backed by lobbyists, Congressional leaders, and think tanks, this project proposes a reactionary counter-revolution against diversity and democratic norms. This is set to be accomplished by implementing policies like expanding the powers of the executive branch to purge those from the government who are not Trump loyalists, dismantling the Department of Education, remodeling the Environmental Protection Agency to cater to the whims of big oil, disempowering the health function of the CDC, eliminating Diversity, Equity, and Inclusion requirements across government departments, and using the Health and Human Services Department to effectively ban abortion on the federal level.

The project also intends to weaponize the military to go after political dissidents; this includes everyone from civilian protesters, members of the media, and anyone who disagrees with the current form of governance. The prime target of this project is the democratic systems that ensure our *right* to have our voices represented in government. Trump is targeting the heart of democracy, *voting*, to cement his power. In 2023 alone, more than 14 states have enacted changes to their voting laws to make it more difficult to participate in the voting process, all of which will go into effect for the 2024 elections. Some of these laws and policies include North Carolina shortening the window for ballot votes, Texas allowing consolidation of polling places, and Nebraska asking for a copy of a Nebraska ID for mail-in ballots. While small at first, these laws will snowball into something much worse that further restricts people's ability to vote. Without the right to speak, organize, and protest, we face a seismic loss of rights that has been unheard of since the founding of this nation. In short, the project is a strategically mapped-out plan to expand the powers of the presidency, exert total control of the government by leveling key departments, and install extremist government officials to oversee the rollout of a deeply fascist order of governance. It is scary to see it spelled out like this. But the only way we can prevent this from becoming our reality is to *vote*. The stakes could not be higher.

And there are differences. Biden and Harris believe in climate change and has pledged to make the American power sector 100% carbon-pollution-free by 2035. With this action, Biden has created the National Climate Task Force, which oversees climate policies. Congress passed the Inflation Reduction Act, which lowers energy costs for families and businesses across the country and increases jobs in clean energy.

Biden and Harris also made remarkable strides in debt forgiveness. The Biden administration has allocated $143 billion to ease or erase the debt of four million Americans within his term. This has not only provided citizens with financial freedom but emotional liberation from the serious toll managing debt can have on an individual and their families. In tandem with debt forgiveness, Biden provided Americans with post-pandemic stimulus packages in order to jumpstart an economy failing because of right-wing, Trumpist policies such as cutting taxes for the very rich.

Finally, one of the most prevalent policies for our generation lies within the reproductive rights of women across the country. While the Supreme Court overturned Roe v. Wade in 2022, the Biden-Harris administration has made consistent strides to ensure that women are supported on a federal and local scale. Biden has supported the FDA initiative for allowing contraceptives such as mifepristone in all states regardless of their local laws. Biden understands that this issue cannot be taken lightly, so he has partnered with Congressmen and Congresswomen such as Hyde-Smith from Michigan and Murray from Washington state to enact and empower the communities that seek for this fundamental right as Americans.

Our generation takes pride in fighting for climate activism, debt forgiveness, and reproductive rights for us and our future citizens. Throughout Biden's term, he and his administration have been actively listening and enacting the changes we hope to see in the country. We must understand that many of these policies also have to go through strenuous obstacles such as Congress, which is full of diverse ages and opinions. Yet, there are some young stars amongst the House of Representatives who can guide Biden to make better choices within our nation and across the world. Some of the advocates include Cori Bush from Missouri, AOC from New York, and Rashida Tlaib from Michigan. These three women have been at the forefront of generational and systemic changes in the United States and abroad, especially in Gaza. These three women are also well-connected and influenced by the demands of our generation and will constantly advocate for these policies despite the constant belittling. We can trust these women will fight relentlessly for the American and Palestinian people. However, if we want even a *chance* to push for policies we care about in the future, this may be our last chance before voting ceases to exist. State and local elections are also just as, if not more, important than the presidential one. Our local and state politicians have the power to check and pressure the president into caring about the policies that actually matter. In the end, go out and vote! There is always more than voting as well: joining a campaign, calling your representative, and most importantly staying politically informed. The other chapters in the book dive deep into the issues that matter in specifics.

Your voice matters just as much as ours.

16 Nuts and Bolts

Registering, Voting, Mobilizing Your Community

Charles Derber, Suren Moodliar, Matt Nelson, and Nancy Treviño

Below we have provided a list of starting points needed to register to vote, receive voting information and alerts, get involved in campaigns, and to support critical causes. This list is by no means comprehensive and is intended to be suggestive of the kinds of resources available.

Register to Vote

Vote.gov
Federal website operated in partnership with the United States Election Assistance Commission

Use this site to register to vote in your state, find registration deadlines, confirm your registration, register after a move, change your party affiliation, and get a voter registration card

Mobilize Other Voters

Vote.org
Non-partisan website to make voting more accessible to voters, especially underserved voters of color and underrepresented young voters

Use this site for registration purposes, to vote by mail, to get reminders, and to learn what's on the ballot
Importantly, it empowers your organization to start its own voter engagement drive

DOI: 10.4324/9781003544371-19

Absentee & Early Voting

NASS.org/can-i-vote/absentee-early-voting
Operated by the National Association of Secretaries of State

You may be eligible to vote prior to the election as an absentee or early voter. State laws vary greatly, so be sure to pay attention to the information provided by your election officials

Use this site to supplement the above sites by selecting your state

County Labor Councils & State Federations

AFL-CIO.org/about-us/our-unions-and-allies/state-federations-and-central-labor-councils
This site is maintained by the American Federation of Labor – Council of Industrial Unions.

Use this site to identify local labor organizations in all 50 states, plus the District of Columbia and Puerto Rico

Voters Rights Organizations

CommonCause.org
This organization has a comprehensive pro-democracy agenda involving legislation, litigation, research, and organizing

Use this site to research issues and get breaking news and alerts. You can also find your closest state-based affiliate

NAACPLDF.org
The Legal Defense Fund uses legal tools, research, narrative construction, and organizing to defend voters of color

Use this site to find local chapters and activists working on voting and racial justice

EmilysList.org
Emily's List works to elect pro-choice women running for office

Use this site to learn about candidates and support their campaigns

Campaigning Organizations
PRESENTE.org
Digital Organizing hub for Latinx communities

Take part in strategic online campaigns designed for maximum and measurable impact.

BlackVotersMatterFund.org
Multi-issue organizing aimed at increasing the power of marginalized, predominantly Black communities.

Volunteer for actions, donate funds, and receive alerts

VotoLatino.org
Multi-issue organizing and electoral activism focused on Latinx communities

Sign up for actions, register to vote and receiving alerts

Electoral.DSAusa.org
Democratic Socialists of
   America's National
   Electoral Commission

Learn which candidates
   and ballot measures
   reflect DSA's working-
   class agenda and join
   campaigns

EvergreenAction.com
Evergreen is a leading
   climate action
   organization

Learn about actions and
   donate to green causes

CodePink.org
CODEPINK is a
   feminist grassroots
   organization working
   to end U.S. warfare
   and imperialism, and
   support peace and
   human rights initiatives

Learn about campaigns,
   major issues of war and
   peace, and how funds
   can be redirected to
   support life-affirming
   programs.
Take actions, sign up for
   alerts, and donate to
   CODEPINK

Part II

The Power of the Electorate – Working with Voters

17 Turning Out Young Voters of Color by Focusing on Their Priority Issue

The Rising Cost of Living

Saru Jayaraman

Numerous polls are showing that young voters and voters of color are naming "the rising cost of living" and "jobs with living wages" as their top priority issues when deciding whether to vote and who to vote for in 2024. In our experience, focusing on this issue and allowing millions of voters in battleground states to "vote themselves a raise" is the best way to motivate them to turn out and vote for candidates who clearly support that raise.

Fortunately, One Fair Wage has a program to do exactly that in multiple key states in 2024. In fact, we are in a moment of historic worker power that could translate into voter power if we focus on what workers are telling us they need. After many years of organizing and building power with hundreds of thousands of restaurant and service workers and "high road" restaurant owners to raise wages and end the subminimum wage for tipped workers, still $2.13 an hour and a direct legacy of slavery, One Fair Wage has documented massive upheaval in the restaurant industry that is driving change. Over one million workers have left the industry, demanding higher wages, and they are winning – thousands of restaurants have raised wages, in some cases dramatically, in order to recruit and retain staff.

To take advantage of this historic moment, One Fair Wage has launched the *25 by 250 campaign*, in which we are working to raise wages and end subminimum wages in 25 states by the United States' 250th Anniversary (2026), with recent victories in Washington, DC and Chicago. We are organizing workers, employers, and coalition partners to advance One Fair Wage as legislative policy in nine states in 2023 and 2024 and lead pivotal ballot measures to do the same in four more states in 2024. Our campaign – and in particular our ballot initiatives – have become even more critical given recent polling showing that the top issue for young people, people of color, and other unlikely voters in 2024 is "the rising cost of living" and "jobs with living wages."[1] *As a result, our campaigns will not only raise wages for 3.5 million workers in 2024; they will also mobilize 350,000 new, unlikely low-wage voters – mostly young people of color – to turn out to "vote themselves*

DOI: 10.4324/9781003544371-21

a raise" this year, and build powerful bases of workers and employers for long-term change.

Background

With nearly 14 million workers, the restaurant industry has been one of the largest and fastest growing sectors of the US economy, and one of the largest employers of youth, women, people of color, immigrants, formerly incarcerated individuals, and many other communities for decades. Forty percent of the 14 million workers are under the age of 24, and the industry has the highest rates of single mothers of any US sector.

Unfortunately, the restaurant industry has also been one of the lowest-paying sectors of the US economy for generations. A legacy of slavery, the subminimum wage for tipped workers, still $2.13 an hour at the federal level, was always a source of poverty, racial inequity, and sexual harassment for millions of service workers nationwide, and a source of liability for restaurant owners. The COVID-19 pandemic exacerbated this crisis. Service workers reported reduced tips and increased customer hostility and as a result, 1.2 million workers have left the industry. In response, thousands of restaurants have voluntarily transitioned to paying a full minimum wage for tipped workers during the pandemic in order to recruit staff.

This upheaval has led us to the precipice of policy change, in which the opposition to raising wages from restaurants has substantially diminished, and there is great momentum for policy change. As a result, we won a 300% wage increase for service workers on the ballot – with a 75% margin! – in Washington, DC on November 8, 2022, and also won a 50% wage increase for 100,000 service workers in the City of Chicago with a 36/10 vote – with many more states to follow.

The massive upheaval in the industry and our impending victories resulting from this change creates enormous opportunity and one of the few silver linings of the pandemic – as well as a vehicle to excite disaffected voters, particularly youth, people of color, and young women of color in particular, in November 2024 and beyond. Our recent victories in DC and Chicago, the 13 states moving One Fair Wage as policy in 2024 and beyond, and this broader national moment of opportunity, will all create momentum for pending federal policy to raise the minimum wage and end the subminimum wage for tipped workers – if we are able to fully take advantage of the moment, as outlined below.

Ballot Measures to Raise Wages, Mobilize Unlikely Voters, and Build Long-Term Power in Michigan, Ohio, and Arizona

We are leading ballot initiatives to raise wages for millions of workers in Michigan, Ohio, and Arizona – three states that are critical for Presidential and Senate races and will have national implications. Our peer-to-peer voter program, using minimum wage as a motivating issue, will result in hundreds of thousands of low-wage workers in each of these states telling each other to "vote ourselves a raise," and vote for candidates who support the raise as a result. In addition, we are conducting large-scale voter registration programs in these three states using minimum wage as the vehicle to stop young people and register them to vote, which is both more effective and more cost-effective than typical voter registration programs. For example, we have been able to register 10,000 new voters in Ohio over a three-month period as a part of signature gathering to raise the wage, at a cost of $14 per voter registration – less than half what typical voter registration programs cost. By using this issue as the mechanism to stop new voters on the street, we will be able to similarly register tens of thousands more new voters in all three states this year.

We have conducted polling and Catalist voter file analysis in our three-state campaign plan that shows that through these initiatives we could drive at least 350,000 new unlikely voters to the polls to vote for Senate candidates who support the wage increases in MI, OH, AZ, and MA.

The Michigan One Fair Wage Initiative

One Fair Wage Action collected 400,000 signatures to put the issue on the ballot in Michigan in November 2018; the Republican-led legislature took it off the ballot and made it law, to keep low-wage workers and workers of color from being motivated to vote, and then reversed it after the election. Despite this reversal, in fall 2018, we used this issue and a peer-to-peer voter program to mobilize voters and saw a 300% increase in voter turnout among all restaurant workers and a 400% increase in voter turnout among youth voters.

In July 2022, MI Court of Claims declared the legislature's "Adopt and Amend" actions unconstitutional. While the Court of Appeals reversed, the issue is now going to the MI Supreme Court, which is likely to agree with the lower court and state that the original law passed – $12 plus tips – is now the law of Michigan, making Michigan the eighth One Fair Wage state in the United States.

Parallel to this process, we have already submitted 600,000 signatures to put a $15 ballot measure on the ballot in Michigan in 2024. The MI Secretary of State declared that we have collected enough signatures to put the issue on the ballot. Thus, the MI legislature will be required by the courts to implement $12 for all workers and will have the opportunity to implement $15 for all workers. If they do implement $15, we will be able to run a large peer-to-peer voter engagement program in 2024 in which low-wage workers are able to tell each other to vote for electeds who delivered a wage increase; if they do not adopt the $15 initiative, we will be able to use our peer-to-peer voter program to turn out tens of thousands of low-wage worker voters who will "vote themselves a raise" and vote for candidates who support it while they are at the ballot box.

The Ohio and Arizona One Fair Wage Ballot Measures

In Ohio and Arizona, we have worked with restaurant workers, unions, and several community partners to raise the state minimum wage and end subminimum wages for tipped workers, workers with disabilities, and youth. Over two million workers in Ohio and Arizona will receive a raise through this ballot measure.

In both states, we have hired hundreds of low-wage workers, particularly restaurant workers, and trained them to collect signatures from their fellow workers. They are conducting voter registration while collecting signatures, at the rate of 1 VR per every 25–30 signatures, and at a cost of $14 per VR. The voter registration program is particularly effective because we are contacting new voters – youth, people of color, single mothers, and others – using minimum wage as the issue that stops them on the street, and then registering them to vote in order to allow them to sign the petition to raise the wage.

We will be developing these worker canvassers as leaders to share their stories and serve as spokespeople for the campaign; in 2024, they will lead the peer-to-peer voter engagement program to win the measure, and after the measures are passed, they will lead the process of implementation in 2025. We are also developing a cadre of restaurant owners across the state who are already paying One Fair Wage or seek to, given the staffing crisis, to also share their stories and uplift their voices in support of the ballot measure.

Numerous studies, outlined below, have demonstrated that while low-wage workers are generally unlikely to vote, putting their highest priority issue – their wages – on the ballot dramatically increases their turnout. This is especially true in 2024, when numerous polls of youth and voters of color show that "the rising cost of living" and "jobs with living wages" are the top issues for voters this year.[2]

The Evidence: Minimum Wage and Voter Turnout Among Low-Wage Workers

Numerous studies over multiple years have shown that putting minimum wage directly on the ballot drives voter turnout. A sample of these studies is outlined below.

Election 2016: Senate Races May Turn on Minimum Wage and Overtime[3]

Perhaps most significantly, the polls showed that when voters weigh candidates' positions on raising the federal minimum wage and expanding overtime pay, support for Republican Senate incumbents declined and support for their Democratic challengers increased, shifting the leads to the Democrats in some races and adding to their leads in others.

More Money, More Turnout? Minimum Wage Increases and Voting[4]

An analysis of county-level panel data from 1980–2016 demonstrates that minimum-wage increases are associated with increases in aggregate voter turnout across many contexts.

The Effect of Signing Ballot Petitions on Turnout[5]

Signing a ballot petition significantly increases the likelihood that the initiative petition signer turns out to vote for the election at which the initiative is placed on the ballot.

One Fair Wage has also experienced this very positive effect of centering minimum wage as an issue to drive unlikely low-wage worker voter turnout, particularly when coupled with a relational (peer-to-peer) voter program in which low-wage workers tell each other to "vote ourselves a raise." In the restaurant industry in particular, we have seen a relational program using the minimum wage as a driving issue work very well because restaurant workers are highly socially networked; they work together, live together, and socialize together across restaurants and thus have strong contacts to encourage to vote, particularly when their wages are at stake.

2018 One Fair Wage Action Relational Voter Turnout Analysis

In 2018, One Fair Wage Action (then called ROC Action) conducted voter engagement with 100,000 low-wage worker voters using minimum wage as the motivating issue and a relational voter engagement program and saw a 300% increase in voter turnout among restaurant workers. We partnered with Analyst Institute to test the effectiveness of our relational voter turnout program as a part of the Directed Research Fund. The Analyst Institute study found our 2018 Relational Voter Turnout program "reached a significantly larger scale than any relational voter turnout program studied with a randomized controlled trial prior to the 2018 cycle" and "appears to have had a potent effect on turnout." In particular, Analyst Institute estimated a VPK of 2.7 voters turned out per thousand dollars spent from that program. Governor Whitmer and the Michigan Democratic Party in 2018 credited restaurant workers for helping win the election.

2022 One Fair Wage Action Relational Voter Turnout Analysis

In 2022 Nevada and 2023 Wisconsin paid relational voter engagement programs led by Empower, One Fair Wage worker members who had in large majority signed a petition to raise the minimum wage responded to relational programs at the highest rate of all the partner groups in the coalition.

The Nevada Research conducted by Empower showed a 2.7% persuasion impact, including a 5% persuasion impact on former Trump voters.[6] The Nevada coalition had 262,000 relational conversations. The Wisconsin program had 530k relational conversations with 300k people in 6 weeks.[7]

One Fair Wage was part of both the Nevada and Wisconsin coalitions. In both states, One Fair Wage had the highest conversion rate of converting its members, who had been recruited through a process of expressing their support for minimum wage increases, to participants in the program, with a 37.6% conversion rate for the list. Most other partners' conversion rates were in single digits. One Fair Wage members were very engaged and key to helping kickstart the program in both WI and NV. One Fair Wage was an invaluable member of the coalition due to our active membership of highly interested tipped workers willing to participate in building lists of fellow tipped workers and allies – largely due to their high rates of social networking.

Notes

1   Celinda Lake, David Mermin, and Emily Garner, *Polling Shows Consistent Support for Raising the Minimum Wage* (Lake Research Partners, January 17, 2024), https://static1.squarespace.com/static/6374f6bf33b7675afa750d48/t/65bd6c4b8e40ce23d0f445af/1706912843958/memo.OFW.v3.f.2024.02.01.pdf.
2   Peter de Guzmsn and Alberto Medina, "Youth and the 2024 Election: Likely to Vote and Ready to Drive Action on Key Political Issues," Center for Information and Research on Civic Learning and Engagement (Center for Information and Research on Civic Learning and Engagement, November 29, 2023), https://circle.tufts.edu/2024-election-youth-poll.
    "Latino Voters Prioritize Inflation and Economy in 2024, New Polling Shows," *MSNBC.com*, November 29, 2023, https://www.msnbc.com/morning-joe/watch/latino-voters-prioritize-inflation-and-economy-in-2024-new-polling-shows-198977605727.

3 Mitchell Hirsch, "Election 2016: Senate Races May Turn on Minimum Wage & Overtime," *NELP Action*, October 2016, https://nelpaction.org/wp-content/uploads /2016/10/Report-Election-2016-Senate-Races-May-Turn-On-Minimum-Wage -Overtime.pdf.
4 Zachary Markovich and Ariel White, "More Money, More Turnout? Minimum Wage Increases and Voting," *The Journal of Politics* 84, no. 3 (July 2022): 1834– 38, https://doi.org/10.1086/716291.
5 Samuel F. Harper and Janine A. Parry, "The Effect of Signing Ballot Petitions on Turnout," *Journal of Elections, Public Opinion and Parties* (November 9, 2023): 1–13, https://doi.org/10.1080/17457289.2023.2281374.
6 "Nevada 2022 Statewide Paid Relational Persuasion Experiment," *Empower Project*, February 1, 2023, https://empowerproject.us/wp-content/uploads/2023 /03/Empower-Project-Nevada-2022-Statewide-Paid-Relational-Persuasion -Experiment-1.pdf.
7 "WI Supreme Court - Empower Project Final Field Report," *Empower Project*, April 10, 2023, https://docs.google.com/document/d/1-IsGK75XZadz5HSktuG -QOR_tnvU3pc7m2iPWYtBCck/.

18 Turning Out Our Peers

Maria Teresa Kumar

I'll cut to the chase: In this age of disinformation and skepticism, the only way to make a real connection with voters is to be undeniably authentic and meet them where they are.

Coming of age in our country in the 80s and 90s, I was always waiting for someone to talk to me in a way that acknowledged my identity as both an American and a Latina. I was either being told that my culture had nothing to do with our democracy or being called upon as a citizen absent any reference to my community.

Despite that, I was lucky enough to develop an interest in politics and democratic work. But so many of my peers never realized the power of their political voice. That is the problem we set out to solve with Voto Latino: showing the young members of our community just how important and valuable they are to our democracy and teaching them that they not only deserve representation but that they have the power to create change.

When we founded the organization 20 years ago, it was an experiment. Plenty of powerful movers and shakers told us that it would never work. Fast forward to the 2020 election, and no one is doubting the power of young Latino voters anymore. We registered more than 650,000 voters in that cycle – turning out an astounding 82% of them to the polls – and mobilized 3.4 million new and low-propensity voters of color.

With our focus on key battleground states including Arizona, Nevada, Georgia, and Pennsylvania, it is fair to say that this cohort of new and energized voters was crucial to the outcomes up and down the ballot. In Arizona, where the Biden-Harris ticket won by just 10,457 ballots, Voto Latino registered 42,260 people and turned out 34,266 of them – 19,263 who were first-time voters.

The key to our success: we understood why so many Latino voters have traditionally stayed on the sidelines. No one was putting forth a consistent and authentic effort to convince them that stepping onto the field was worth their time. Maybe once every four years, someone from Washington or the state capital would show up in their community and tell them that one party

DOI: 10.4324/9781003544371-22

has their backs, but then they would disappear after Election Day with scant evidence of representation throughout the ensuing terms.

The result has been a wide gap in registration and participation between Latino voters and other demographics. Even with all the work we have done in the last 20 years, there are still approximately 20 million eligible Latino voters who did not cast a ballot in the last presidential election.

But our accomplishments at Voto Latino are undeniable proof that the gaps in political participation can be closed. Our recipe for doing so is simultaneously straightforward and the most difficult for both longtime and neophyte political operations to replicate: We have built a lengthy and unimpeachable track record of authenticity, and our community trusts us when we tell them their vote can make a difference.

From the very beginning, we have operated under the principle that our audience is our peer group. If you were to walk down the halls of Voto Latino, you would see folks from various Latino backgrounds and generations. We are members of the very same communities we are speaking with, and we stay in constant contact with them through social and other digital channels.

Our strategy derives from our fierce and deeply held belief in our community. We trust that they will listen to those who credibly represent them, we trust that they will understand their latent political power, and we trust that they will use their voices to strengthen our democracy. And over the last 20 years, we have been able to demonstrate that trust is well placed: of the eight states that we have worked in, Latinos have contributed to flipping five of them.

In turn, we are obsessed with strengthening the trust that our community has in us by meeting them where they are – on the platforms they use and the topics they care about. In 2020, that led to over half a billion high-quality digital impressions that drove turnout far in excess of the rate for Latinos as a whole. By taking this active approach to communication, we have amassed a monthly audience of three million users across social media platforms and a constituency of close to four million people.

To be clear, this dynamic is not a one-way stream of messaging. We are engaged in a back-and-forth conversation with our community. We owe it to them to prove why we deserve their trust by highlighting, supporting, and advocating for the issues that inspire their political participation.

That's why we have been ardent supporters of involving Latino lawmakers in Congressional talks around immigration, and why we launched our ¡Adiós, Sinema! Campaign in 2022 to hold Sen. Kyrsten Sinema accountable for her obstruction of critical voting reforms that would have protected the rights of millions of Latino voters. Authenticity means we are there to laugh, cry, and fight alongside our community – no matter how soon the next election is.

A key component of our approach is that we don't register someone and then hand them off to some other organization to give them a text message on Election Day. Nor do we encourage someone to visit the ballot box and then wish them a happy next three years. As I always say: We like to think of ourselves as a good date – we call you the next day.

That all begs the question of how activists, campaigns, and donors can maximize their impact in the face of this year's all-important election. Certainly, a multi-decade record of authentic and direct communication is unattainable for any operation that only got off the ground after President Biden came into office. The solution, then, is to invest in and partner with the organizations that have already built that requisite trust with their communities.

As the technologies, messages, and strategies of politics change from cycle to cycle, that trust is the essential infrastructure around which our democracy will thrive.

19 1964's Freedom Summer Offers a Model for the Voting Rights Work We Need to Do

Charles Derber

I was part of Freedom Summer in 1964. Sixty years later, with voting rights under attack, I see how we need another.

The day after I graduated from college, I jumped into a car with my room-mate and another friend and headed south to Mississippi. We were in good spirits after graduation, but we were in a racially integrated car, and we sensed danger on the road. A year earlier, three young people with the same destination for the same reason in the same season had been shot and killed. That had been the worst tragedy of what we now celebrate as Freedom Summer.

Freedom Summer, 1964, was a landmark civil rights project to bring multi-racial democracy to a state infamous for its racism and violent denial of Black voting rights. Organized by the Student Nonviolent Coordinating Committee (SNCC) and the Congress of Racial Equality (CORE), and led by the legend-ary civil rights activist Bob Moses, Freedom Summer brought hundreds of Black and white young people into mainly rural areas all over Mississippi. The main goal was to register thousands of Black people to vote and to end Confederate fascism -- a system of caste or race-based tyranny that prevented democracy before the Civil War and was resurrected in the Jim Crow regime after Reconstruction.

Freedom Summer tried to register about 17,000 Black voters, but only 1,600 were accepted by the white registrars. Mississippi politicians and elec-tion officials, alongside the Ku Klux Klan, violently resisted. Two white civil workers, Michael Schwerner and Andrew Goodman, arrived in Mississippi in mid-June 1964, exactly a year before I arrived with my friends. Schwerner and Goodman met James Chaney, a local Black activist who worked with them, but the three disappeared while investigating a church burning. They were found murdered a few weeks later, memorialized on August 4, 1964, by Martin Luther King Jr., who had come to Mississippi and described the deaths as "an attack on the human brotherhood taught by all the great religions of mankind."

Freedom Summer helped unleash a major effort to bring democracy to Mississippi. Voting rights were seen as part of an educational, economic, and political transformation. Voting rights activists helped establish 41 Freedom

DOI: 10.4324/9781003544371-23

Schools for more than 3,000 young Black people, helping provide literacy, history, and organizing skills that would allow the struggle to continue.

It would take my Freedom Summer in 1965 to move closer to the first new phase of multi-racial democracy. In that summer, I lived with a Black family for several months and continued the voting rights and education work begun in 1964. Like the 1964 workers, we faced constant violence, were arrested by the police on the first day, and followed by armed men who once managed to get into our car and tried to strangle us. Despite this violence, we succeeded in registering thousands of new Black voters, and in 1965 we had won enough national support that President Lyndon B. Johnson signed the Civil Rights Act before summer's end. It was the most comprehensive voting rights act passed since Reconstruction, outlawing "abridgement" or "denial" of voting rights to any racial or minority group in every state.

I never imagined then that 60 years later, we would desperately need another Freedom Summer, this time to create a multi-racial democracy across not just the South but the entire nation. Once again, we face election denialism, white Christian nationalism, and a revived American fascism. We need Freedom Summer more urgently than 60 years ago, because in 2024 we face an election that could be our last – and it will take years of new Freedom Summers to win and get real democracy.

Fortunately, civil rights groups, voting registration and turnout campaigns, educators, and social justice activists have begun to seize the moment. The memory of Freedom Summer is helping inspire a new surge of multi-racial voting rights and "democracy movements." Today, two different organizations inspired by Freedom Summer are applying its lessons for the long term.

Black Voters Matter (BVM) embodies Freedom Summer's belief in the power that can be tapped among the most disenfranchised Americans. Like SNCC, Black Voters Matter is a voting rights "democracy movement" rooted in the Deep South. Two Black activists, LaTosha Brown and Cliff Albright, founded BVM in 2016 after years of experience in community organizing, civil rights, and get-out-the-vote pro-democracy activism.

Brown's 1998 youthful race for office in Alabama was targeted by local racist sheriffs, who impounded many of her votes and "forgot" to count them, leaving her "feeling so powerless" in a rigged election. She soon began to realize "how common it was to … steal these elections … and no one was held accountable," according to the *Harvard Gazette*.[1] She was going to change all that.

BVM created the Movement Voting Project (MVP) to turn out 2024 voters in nine key swing states, 40 of the most competitive House districts, and key down-ballot races involving control of state legislatures. What is most reminiscent of Freedom Summer is the fervent grass-roots philosophy and optimism. Many of today's seemingly powerless Southern rural Black communities have "remnants of the civil rights movement" that help inspire current activism, Brown wrote for *The New York Times*.[2] She noted that BVM's local partners in the rural Deep South are often Black women who know their community well and have the ties and know-how to motivate their neighbors to become voting activists.

Brown talks about SNCC in her work – emphasizing in her *Times* piece that you can't "parachute in" but really have to get engaged with local folks to make a difference. This is what Freedom Summer did; I lived with a Black family for the entire summer and got to know their circle. As a community and civil rights organizer, Brown clearly loves the Freedom Summer model and understands that the way to mobilize voters is to join in and know their culture.

Brown also evokes Freedom Summer with her belief in "letting folks know that they are loved and that they matter," reported the *Harvard Gazette*. "We don't come to our community members like they are just votes to be rounded up or counted like jelly beans. We're coming in as friends, with hugs and love." Quoting Martin Luther King, she says, "we always tell people 'Power at its best is love implementing the demands of justice.'"

Democracy Summer is another current voter and democracy movement inspired by Freedom Summer. It was founded by Maryland Congressman Jamie Raskin, a constitutional lawyer known for his leadership in Congress against Trump's January 6 coup attempt. Raskin has put together a multi-racial voting rights campaign focusing on young people who remind me of my fellow activists 60 years ago. They are bursting with fervor to create a real democracy in the US freed from caste and class, and they have mobilized an all-out struggle to defeat Trump and MAGA in 2024 and beyond.

One of the earliest teachers at Democracy Summer was Bob Moses, a 1960s Freedom Summer legend. Moses helped SNCC create the many "freedom schools" run by Freedom Summer. Before he died in 2017, Moses bequeathed to Democracy Summer his updated voter rights and democracy curriculum for the newest generation.

Raskin is focused on economic democracy as well as political democracy. He has not only brought in teachers like civil rights heroes John Lewis and Marc Elias, today's most prominent voting rights lawyer, but labor leaders from the AFL-CIO and the Labor Heritage Foundation, who teach about the labor movement as foundational in building democracy. This is a curriculum focused on both the caste and class hurdles to democracy, an idea animating SNCC and taught by Martin Luther King, who was assassinated while marching with striking garbage workers in Memphis in 1968.

After founding Democracy Summer as part of his 2006 campaign for state senate in Maryland, Raskin decided in 2018 that, as Trump and MAGA rose, his new "democracy school" had to take place every summer to help build "a full-blown pro-democracy, pro-voting rights" curriculum. By the summers of 2021 and 2022, Democracy Summer expanded to partner with more than 100 democracy and voting organizations and recruited over 1,000 high school and college students for summer democracy school. The students became community organizers, realizing they can only win if they address issues vital in their community, from labor to health care to feminism and antiracism.

As a Freedom Summer graduate, I can relate to a graduate of Democracy Summer who testified, "Democracy Summer was truly my most life-changing experience yet. I now hope and aspire to stay continuously politically active…"

BVM and Democracy Summer are just two of many pro-democracy campaigns rising for 2024 and the long term. Among the activists invited to speak at Democracy Summer are the Rev. William Barber, the founder of the modern Poor People's Campaign originally started by Martin Luther King. In the spirit of Freedom Summer, Barber organized in 2022 a huge non-violent March of Low Wage Workers on Washington and to the Polls, "targeting the red lights of closed polling places and redistricting and all forms of voter suppression," as reported by *Common Dreams*.[3] The Poor People's Campaign's March to the Polls built an even larger scale campaign for 2024 and beyond, based on Barber's view that the road to victory "goes through the 140 million poor and low-income people," as quoted by *Common Dreams*.

This pro-democracy agenda was joined by the AFL-CIO and the United Auto Workers (UAW), who carry out their own Freedom Summer-style voting rights campaigns for the long term, as do major pro-democracy and voting groups, such as the Progressive Turnout Project and MoveOn.

In Mississippi, it was so hot when I was organizing that I saw Coke machines on most people's porches, where I rushed to quench my thirst. The Mississippi weather and politics were scorching hot. Climate change and MAGA politics have brought the same scorched earth and political terrain; the new 21st-century Freedom Summers will all be hot in both senses.

Young people will face heat – rising temperatures and fascist ghosts packing heat – the rest of their lives. I now teach these students, but I love them as I did when I was one of them. And I have confidence that they will turn out in large numbers and find the same meaning in their fight for democracy, love, and survival that I did in the first Freedom Summer.

Notes

1 Christina Pazzanese, "Black Voters Take the Wheel," *Harvard Gazette*, February 17, 2021, https://news.harvard.edu/gazette/story/2021/02/record-turnout-of-black-voters-comes-after-decades-of-activism/.

2 LaTosha Brown and Cliff Albright, "Opinion | How to Turn a Person Into a Voter," *The New York Times*, October 27, 2018, sec. Opinion, https://www.nytimes.com/2018/10/27/opinion/voter-voting-alabama-black.html.

3 Jake Johnson, "Poor People's Campaign Readies 'Massive, Nonviolent' Effort to Save Democracy," *Common Dreams*, January 15, 2022, https://www.commondreams.org/news/2022/01/15/poor-peoples-campaign-readies-massive-nonviolent-effort-save-democracy.

20 Mobilizing with Elder Voters

Akaya Windwood and Bill McKibben

The 2024 elections will be a referendum on democracy – so perhaps it's good that Americans with a long history of living in one will play a key role in determining its outcome.

We at Third Act, the group we helped form in 2021, think older Americans are beginning to turn in the progressive direction, a turn that will accelerate as time goes on.

A lot has been written about the impact of young voters in November's contests, and rightly so. The enormous margins that Democrats ran up among voters under 30 let them squeak through in race after race. Progressives should be incredibly grateful that the next generation can see straight through Trumpism in a way that too many of their elders can't.

But there were also intriguing hints of what looked like a gray countercurrent that helped dampen the expected red wave. Yes, older people by and large voted Republican, in keeping with what political scientists have long insisted: that we become more conservative as we age. But in the 63 most competitive congressional districts, the places where big money was spent on ads and where the margin in the House was decided, polling by AARP, an advocacy group for people over 50, found some fascinating numbers.[1]

In early summer, Republicans had a sturdy lead among older voters in 50 of those districts, up 50 percent to 40 percent. This had Republicans salivating. But on Election Day, voters over 65 actually broke for Democrats in those districts, 49 to 46.

That doesn't surprise us at Third Act. We've learned that our demographic is far less settled than people sometimes suppose.

Some of the issues that benefited Democrats are obvious, of course. Republican messaging included calls for weakening Social Security and Medicare even though most older beneficiaries rely on Social Security for most of their income, and for an estimated 40 percent, it's all their retirement income.[2] The cruelty of toying with people's life support systems is matched only by its political foolishness. Among voters 65 and over, Social Security and Medicare were among the top concerns.

DOI: 10.4324/9781003544371-24

But something else happened, too. When the Supreme Court tossed out Roe v. Wade in early summer, most of the pictures were of young women protesting, appropriately, since it's their lives that will be turned upside down. But people we know in their 60s and 70s felt a real psychic upheaval: A woman's right to choose had been part of their mental furniture for five decades. And they've lived their entire lives in what they had imagined was a stable and working democracy.

The top concern to voters 65 and over, especially women, was "threats to democracy," according to AARP. And exit polling by the Kaiser Family Foundation found that among women 50 and older, the court's decision overturning the constitutional right to abortion had a major impact on which candidate they supported.[3] Sixty-six percent of Black women said so, as did 61 percent of Hispanic women and 48 percent of white women. Voters who said the Supreme Court's abortion decision was the single most important factor in their vote supported Democrats two to one.

And would it surprise you to learn that, according to 2023 data from the Environmental Voter Project, older voters trail only the youngest cohort in their concern for the climate? The numbers are astonishing: In Arizona and Pennsylvania – two crucial swing states in 2024 – the populations of older climate voters are so large that they make up 4.8 percent and 4.7 percent, respectively, of the entire electorate in each state.

Some of our members helped organize access to abortion before Roe was decided in 1973; they don't want to go back. And it's not only abortion: The Supreme Court also took on the Clean Air Act of 1970 and the Voting Rights Act of 1965. We helped win these fights once, turning out by the tens of millions to oppose the war in Vietnam or for the first Earth Day. And we can help win them again – we have the muscle memory of what organizing on a large scale feels like.

Hundreds of us from around the country converged on Nevada in the days before the midterm vote because we determined – correctly, as it turned out – that it might be the place where control of the Senate would be decided.[4] We may walk a tad slower door to door, but in this case, slow and steady helped to win the race.

And we've helped win big battles since. This past autumn, Third Act teamed up behind the frontline activists on the Gulf of Mexico to demand a pause in permitting for huge new LNG export facilities. We wrote thousands of handwritten letters to the Department of Energy (we spent a lot of time learning penmanship once upon a time) and we signed up by the hundreds for a sit-in outside the Department of Energy in rocking chairs – a sit-in that we got to call off when the Biden administration did the right thing with two weeks to spare.

We know that young people have been in the lead in this fight, because they'll have to live with the world we're creating. But as long as we're still here, we'll have to live with the knowledge of what we're leaving behind, so we want to change it while we still can.

We recognize that this will require a sustained effort beyond the next election and the election after that. Numerous analysts and demographers believe that coming demographic changes in the United States will generally favor Democrats. But complications abound. Partisan gerrymandering continues to favor Republicans, for instance, and at least five states that generally vote Democratic have each lost a seat from their congressional delegations.[5]

But here's the thing. Many of us are going to be here for quite a while. Ten thousand Americans turn 60 every day, and on average we'll live an additional 23 years. The last of the baby boomers will be 65 or older in 2030. Youth voters, moreover, are youth voters for only about a decade.[6] One guarantee for 2024: We'll vote in huge numbers, as we always do. One possibility is that we'll help turn back the clock a little, toward the world we actually built in our youth.

We're not your parents' grandparents.

Notes

1 "AARP Poll of 63 Most Competitive Congressional Districts Shows Older Voters Were the Deciders in 2022," *MediaRoom*, November 17, 2022, https://press.aarp .org/2022-11-17-AARP-Post-Election-Survey.

2 Jim Tankersley, "Republicans, Eyeing Majority, Float Changes to Social Security and Medicare," *The New York Times*, November 2, 2022, sec. U.S., https://www .nytimes.com/2022/11/02/us/politics/republicans-social-security-medicare.html.

   "Fact Sheet - Social Security" (Washington, DC: Social Security Administration, 2024).

   Kelly Kenneally, "New Report: 40% of Older Americans Rely Solely on Social Security for Retirement Income," *National Institute on Retirement Security* (blog), January 14, 2020, https://www.nirsonline.org/2020/01/new-report-40-of-older -americans-rely-solely-on-social-security-for-retirement-income/.

3 Ashley Kirzinger et al., "How The Supreme Court's Dobbs Decision Played in 2022 Midterm Election: KFF/AP VoteCast Analysis," *KFF* (blog), November 11, 2022, https://www.kff.org/other/poll-finding/2022-midterm-election-kff-ap-vote-cast-analysis/.

4 Shiela Leslie, "Opinion: She Had the Most Endangered Seat in the US Senate. Here's How She Held onto It," CNN, November 14, 2022, https://www.cnn.com /2022/11/14/opinions/election-deniers-2022-senate-nevada-cortez-masto-leslie/ index.html.

5 "New Congressional Districts Created after the 2020 Census," *Ballotpedia*, accessed June 5, 2024, https://ballotpedia.org/New_congressional_districts_cre-ated_after_the_2020_census.

6 US Census Bureau, "2020 Census Will Help Policymakers Prepare for the Incoming Wave of Aging Boomers," *Census.gov*, accessed June 5, 2024, https:// www.census.gov/library/stories/2019/12/by-2030-all-baby-boomers-will-be-age -65-or-older.html.

21 Restoring Democracy through Our Public Schools

Helen Gym

Across the country, voters are turning their eyes away from Washington and back to the places where politics make a difference – at home, in local elections, and on issues that keep our families healthy and safe. That's why energizing our elections by putting the public back in public education matters now more than ever.

One thing is certain. The furious attacks on education – from book bans to anti-LGBT laws to the erosion of DEI and affirmative action – mirror a larger backlash to gains made in racial progress, voting rights, and labor organizing. Attacks on education serve as proxy battles to undermine our commitment to the public good and point to larger threats to our democracy. In state after state where public education is under attack, we have seen concurrent rollbacks on voting rights and freedoms. The battlegrounds of race, culture, and democracy have shifted from voting booths to school libraries, university boardrooms, and school board meetings. These attacks have been well funded and organized; the fight for quality schools and education justice must be more so.

Public schools, flawed and under siege as they are, remain one of the most aspirational spaces from which to launch a counter to the forces of privatization and disinvestment and to activate diverse constituencies to effectuate large-scale government and societal change. Putting communities front and center means we prioritize the voices of parents, community members, educators, and young people who demand that schools become spaces of affirmation, humanity, and possibility. When we organize around our schools, we learn to build multiracial coalitions rooted in education as a common good and where public will and civic engagement are essential to a healthy, vibrant school system and core to a stronger, stable society and democracy. Not only do we counter forces of disinvestment, but we reach a broader audience to improve public and civil discourse, expand democratic practices and principles in public forums and spaces, and expand the voices of once marginalized communities exhorting for progress and change.

This is something I have not only witnessed, but through years of organizing and investing in educational justice, I helped win a healthier, stronger politics. I spent two decades as one of Philadelphia's leading community

DOI: 10.4324/9781003544371-25

organizers, building power and voice among our city's immigrant rights and education organizing communities. As a former teacher and parent, I founded a citywide parents' organization that challenged a 17-year state takeover of our schools; forged coalitions with librarians, cafeteria workers, and bus drivers; and took on yearly budget cuts and mass school closings.

These movements brought me into the Philadelphia City Council in 2016 when local office was the last refuge for communities to challenge the privatization and defunding of schools. From there, we proved that elected officials working hand in hand with organizing communities could do more than win elections. We could effectuate lasting change in investments. Not only did we end the state takeover, but we restored nurses, counselors, and arts programs in schools. We centered health care and mental health supports amid the COVID crisis, and we led a $500 million school modernization campaign to bring clean water and air conditioning to classrooms.

As the Co-Chair of Local Progress, a national network of municipal elected officials committed to racial and economic justice, I've seen our work to mobilize and train school board members expand exponentially – especially as they face off against moneyed interests.

Take Central Bucks School District in Pennsylvania. In 2022, the school board made national headlines for allegedly violating LGBT student rights and passing restrictive policies against speech or materials that advocated for any social policy or partisan point of view. This included one principal threatening disciplinary action against a teacher who had posted a quote by Nobel Peace laureate and author Elie Wiesel.

Students, educators, and parents got activated, and in a sweeping election threw out a GOP majority that had passed those very policies. Two remaining GOP board members later resigned. Many of the new school board members were first-time candidates motivated to action and focused on teacher retention, mental health, and combating learning loss post-pandemic.

"This is a victory for our students, our teachers, our support staff, and our community," wrote new School Board President Karen Smith.

With this vote, we showed that love is stronger than hate and compassion is stronger than fear. And voters made clear they will not be divided or distracted from working together – all of us – to solve the real issues facing all of our students.[1]

What the Central Bucks School District fight shows is that public education continues to resonate in every state, including states that the Democratic party has lost over the decades. Look at the success of the 2019 statewide teacher strikes in Oklahoma, West Virginia, Arizona, and Kentucky. Fair pay for teachers kickstarted conversations about wealth inequality, the gender wage gap, and the state of our middle class.

As I wrote in 2020, voters don't hew to any particular ideology when it comes to their children's lives. When people see a neighborhood school close down because of budget cuts, when they lose a school nurse or worry over learning loss, they take action.

When an issue is seen as a crisis in which their own children's lives are at stake, voters care less about what end of the ideological spectrum we're on than whether we're protecting and offering real solutions for their children. When we involve teachers, nurses, librarians, and school counselors at the door, voters move even closer toward us.

The most effective campaigns do three things. First, they center a message about the power of public schools to move us closer to a unified community. The appalling efforts of certain political factions to scapegoat vulnerable communities in order to distract from disinvesting in our schools run afoul with what most Americans demand: real investments in their children and maintaining the fundamental mission of schools to shape engaged, educated, and democratic citizens.

Second, successful campaigns broaden and activate the constituencies most impacted by school disinvestment. When Pennsylvania, Wisconsin, Ohio, and Texas moved to limit collective bargaining, public school educators became a highly mobilized political force in local elections. As we work to GOTV in communities that are often tuned out of and turned off by political candidates, public school teachers, counselors, nurses, and educators become crucially important and respected GOTV partners.

Third, successful education-based campaigns are about concrete solutions that address academic success, human dignity, and community safety and opportunity. The right-wing culture wars do little to address parents' fears about learning loss in schools. Expanding nurses and counselors, school support staff, renovating libraries, and creating community schools with vibrant extracurricular programs do.

Few things illustrate gross inequity more than the difference between a modern school building in a wealthy neighborhood and a crumbling school in an underfunded school district. Use the fact that most schools are polling locations to drive home the close connection between public education and reinvestment. Our school buildings are a means to build, modernize, and invest in every neighborhood – not just downtowns, ports, and business centers. When we build schools, we create jobs and build the cities and towns of our future.

No matter what you choose to talk about, in every election, our movement must come to the ballot box with a mandate for equity and transformative change.

The stakes couldn't be higher in the 2024 election.

Let's make sure voters see themselves, their families, and their future in the voting booth and in our politics.

Note

1 Isabela Dias, "Pennsylvania Voters Rejected the Culture Wars in School Board Races," *Mother Jones* (blog), accessed June 5, 2024, https://www.motherjones .com/politics/2023/11/pennsylvania-voters-rejected-the-culture-wars-in-school -board-races-bucks-county-moms-for-liberty/.

22 Working with Labor Movement Voters

Mark Spadafore

*This conversation ranges from the benefits of a more progressive regula-
tory state to the bread-and-butter conversations that happen within trade
union memberships and broader communities of working people.*

—The Editors

*Editors: In some quarters, organizing among workers is prioritized in a way
that is indifferent to electoral politics. Does having a fairly responsive
federal government help, or is that immaterial to the needs of workers?*
Mark Spadafore: Absolutely. I mean, that's the thing that … it's hard to get
people excited about the administrative state. People don't remember this.
On the first day that Joe Biden was inaugurated, one of the first things he
did was fire the General Counsel of the National Labor Relations Board.
It's the one thing that he kind of went in and muscled through, and he
put pro-labor people on the NLRB. I think you saw this in the 1930s
too. We're comparing a lot to that time in history. But then, you saw a
lot of organizing and militancy among the working class because of the
Depression. Then, you saw the creation, under the Wagner Act/National
Labor Relations Act, of the administrative process for people to form
unions. You had all these things coming together all at once, and I think
you're seeing a version of that now.

It's not perfect by any stretch of the imagination. Instead of the depression,
it was the pandemic. I do think and feel that it's a combination of the two
that has allowed all of this to happen. You can show it, because you can see
the pushback now. You have SpaceX and Amazon and Trader Joe's. They're
trying to basically upend the National Labor Relations Act. I think if they get
the courts, it's going to be overturned because this is a court that doesn't care
about precedent, doesn't care about the administrative state. In fact, there's
the other case, the Disproportionate Share Hospital payments, that allows the
Department of Health and Human Services to interpret Medicare benefits.
There's a specific rule that is before the Supreme Court, and everybody thinks
it's going to be overturned there. Basically, they want to take down the ability

DOI: 10.4324/9781003544371-26

of the federal government to enforce any regulations. We have to understand at the end of the day, after all the cultural war stuff, it really comes down to economics.

Editors: *When you think about partisanship and having taken us to the economic piece of it, when you talk with your union members and the broader public about issues, especially the overall political circumstances, how do you connect their immediate concerns and the political circumstances? Are there stories from your organizing work that would illustrate to us, who are not directly involved in union work, how we should be talking with people?*

Mark: To just answer that question: Here is where the American labor movement is, and this is one of the inherent weaknesses: it's all tied around the collective bargaining agreement, which is both good and bad in many ways. The conversations we have to have are varied, especially for our membership. In my 1199 work, we represent private sector healthcare workers – everything from hospitals, nursing homes, home-care workers, personal care assistants, all the way up to nurse practitioners – in the gamut of healthcare. We tend to be a union of mostly women of color, but we also have members in rural areas. Places like Gouverneur, Carthage, and places like that, which are not people of color. It's mostly women, but it's mostly rural white women. When having political conversations, we do have to code-switch a little bit. Having a conversation in Buffalo, Rochester, or Syracuse, which are inner cities, is different than having those conversations in places like Carthage, Corning, Gouverneur, or more rural places.

With labor, it's always a little different; it doesn't serve us to be tied to the partisan arguments. The issue arguments, *yes.* Here's a good example. This is happening right now on the state-budget level. Long story short, our members' salaries are paid by and large by the Medicaid program. The other part of it is paid for by Medicare. Even though it's federal money, it's controlled by the State of New York. So every year, we tend to have these big budget fights to ensure that we have funding. It's the second-largest piece of the New York State budget, right after education. There's always this tendency on the part of most governors: "Well, we need to rein in the cost of Medicaid!" Because it is an expensive program. And in New York, we have a very robust program. We have the largest Medicaid budget. I think California's might be more than ours now, but we're bigger than Texas and Florida, even though they have more people than we do, because we fund more services with it. New York's always kind of used this as a way to make sure we're expanding access to care across the state, and especially for the people who don't have health insurance or are indigent. So it's a very robust program. Many of the hospitals and nursing homes depend on that funding. Having that conversation with our members, we have to draw that line from there to why you need to be involved in the political process.

Many of our rural members are very taken by the Trump message – especially the way the message plays on resentment. You know, resentment of people in cities, resentment of people of color – all of those things that play along with perceptions of identity. For us, in this budget fight this year, we're fighting the governor, a Democratic woman governor, actually. We have a good conversation there now. It's like, "Yes, we're fighting the governor that, by the way, you don't like either. Fine, neither do we. Here's why you need to be involved ..." And then we move from partisanship to the issue.

That's been a good conversation to have. And so on the issue stuff, we can have conversations with our more conservative members because we can draw that line directly to the paycheck. We *also* start to get beyond that. That's where the conversation in our rural areas gets a little trickier. I would also say it's trickier in some ways in our urban areas because everybody assumes that if you're a person of color, you're this big progressive. Some imagine that if you're a Black or brown person, that necessarily means that you're all on board with the gun safety agenda. But a lot of our members of color have guns because they don't feel safe.

They all have stories of how police have harassed them, but they're not "defund-the-police." They're like, "Yes, I know the people who would come and take my stuff in my neighborhood," especially considering the way that the police do the maintenance of redlined areas. People tend to depend on that. They're like, "No, I *want* to have the police there to protect me."

Having those conversations, it doesn't fall into the larger political narrative because a larger political narrative, especially in America, is very much like sports. Who's up, who's down? There's no context to anything. I think that for us, the challenge has to be trying to draw out that conversation so it doesn't turn into this "who is up, who is down" mode. The Trump message is very simplistic, it's visceral and emotional. But feelings are not wrong in my opinion. The facts that base your feelings might be wrong, but the feelings are not wrong. How you feel, there's a reason why you feel that way. The problem is that most people don't turn around and figure out, "All right, why do we feel this way?"

Editors: *Do you find that in the context of your work, you're able to create situations for these kinds of conversations? Or is it simply too challenging, too time-consuming?*

Mark: Well, it's my job, so we have to do it. We have no choice. We tried to do a monthly political discussion, check-in with special speakers, stuff like that. We couldn't sustain it. It was very hard to do. And we did many things virtually during the pandemic. The good thing about the pandemic is that we did open up this virtual world, this virtual piece.

Taking off my 1199 hat and putting on my labor council hat: my thing is to insist that meetings should be hybrid, in person-online. I'll give you a great example. We had a meeting, or we have our monthly delegate meeting, and one of the delegates was in Washington. Their union had a conference down there and literally was on his phone at the steps of the Lincoln Memorial.

Some people are like, "I don't like this hybrid. You're always turning your back," because it is challenging. I have the monitor here, I've got people here. I'm always doing this because I don't want to turn my back on the people on camera. I don't want to turn my back too much on people in the room. But I said to some of those people, "You see? That's why we do this. You could be at the Lincoln Memorial and still participate here." And what I hope it does is open up the possibilities for people to think. It's a member organization, but I want to make sure that we're reaching beyond the membership, not just the same old people in the room. We have to be thinking always. And I think that we need to be thinking about how we can craft a message so that we reach those people in the broader public. For example, it used to be in New York that you had the Rockefeller Republicans. And we had to have a message that would also attract them. Many of those Rockefeller Republicans are now Democrats, mainstream Democrats. It shows you how far to the right everything has moved. And that's why when people talk about, "Well, the extreme left," I'm like, "They used to be the mainstream left back in the day." And you do have some people who have really radical thoughts and things like that, but by and large, they're still operating within the framework of democracy. That's the thing that makes the right-wing extremes so extreme – they don't want to operate within the framework. They're about getting rid of the framework and just having totalitarian fascism.

As much as I respect, and in some ways love, our constitution, the way that the courts are now – Thank you, Mitch McConnell! Thank you, Federalist Society! It's everything that they have planned from the 1960s on because they were so afraid of socialism. And this shapes the conversations we have with members and the public. In response to this fear of the public sector, I often turn around and say, "We have socialized trash collection." I mean, come on. So at the end of the day, that's what really worries me, and having those conversations with members is critical. Some of my members are getting it now. We're discussing things like Project 2025; how do we use that? I don't know if that's too in the weeds. But the threat is right there. You just use Trump's own words. Some will say, "Well, he's just talking." And it's like, "No, he's not!" Everyone heard by now. He means what he says.

Editors: *We're certain that he means much of what he says. If you look at something as mundane as weather reporting, which depends on several federal agencies, Trump managed to really compromise that system in favor of small-scale private interests – these multimillionaires who run small outfits are able to climb in and advance their interests. We're really worried about that too. But let's take an ordinary person who is concerned, who is troubled, and wants to mobilize their friends and family. Let's say they're in New York and they're concerned about mobilizing friends in Pennsylvania, in Michigan. How would they go about doing that as ordinary individuals? Who would they have to partner with? Who would they have to turn to?*

Mark: Well, it's funny because for us, a lot of times we do tend to go down to Pennsylvania on the labor side, and that's taken our members, again, it's membership-based, down to Pennsylvania to do these larger mobilizations. So for us, it is this larger piece. On the other hand, if you're not a union member, to get to your question, what can you do? I mean, I know there are groups out there where you can do postcards, and I think they do have a calling system, and there's the online stuff like MoveOn does and groups like that. But it isn't like you have this place that you can automatically plug into. That's the reason why on the labor side, we still have the power – we have the resources to plug in everyday people. I mean, that's the thing. It's like everybody thinks that union members, again, are these big progressive folks; they're not. We reflect the larger public, depending on our field.

So if you're a construction worker, I mean, because of the construction industry, it's often, as some people joke, "pale, male, and stale." That's who they are. That's what it is. And I'll say this, I mean, it's funny, we're doing a lot of work in the primary with a former teacher union president running for Congress. The carpenters were saying, "Yes, we have about a hundred and some odd people that can vote in this primary." Whereas in my union, we have about 4,000 that can vote in this primary. So we have a much bigger group because of basically demography. So numbers matter when we strategize about mobilization.

Therefore, there are challenges for the average person to plug into larger unions. Groups like Indivisible, I think, have done a good job of plugging in and connecting to those larger entities. MoveOn also does this to a certain extent, although they kind of wax and wane depending on what's going on with them. But by and large, you have to find these other groups that do that, like the Sierra Club. There's others too. There's Black Voters Matter. They tend to focus more on the South, but that's what I mean. It's like you have all these groups, and this is the weakness of the left. It's too decentralized. That's why labor is so powerful. We have a centralized structure: "Here, you can plug in here!"

Editors: When you take your members, or when your members go with you, to another state, say to Pennsylvania, to knock on doors, is that an educational experience for them? Are they more active in the union afterward? How does that work?

Mark: Yes, I would say that ... It definitely is a bonding experience depending on what happens. Look, last time we went down – obviously, we didn't go down in 2020 because of the pandemic, but in 2016 we went – that was a big lesson for us because Pennsylvania went for Trump, and we saw it. We saw the energy around Trump that we did not see here in New York state because Trump's message just doesn't resonate here. But in Pennsylvania, James Carville's famous remark about Pennsylvania, "it's Philadelphia, Pittsburgh, and Alabama right in the middle," rings true in a lot of ways. When we were in the city of Scranton, we were okay. When we took one step outside the city, we went off of a political cliff.

Editors: We really appreciate your frank comments about the challenges and the way in which the message resonate in particular communities. To conclude, can you provide us with some insights into your organizing career?

Mark: Oh my God! How far do you want to go back? [Laughs] I mean, I've been doing this work for over 30 years. I started working at Syracuse Labor Council in 1998. I worked there for 10 years. I actually started a small not-for-profit to work on community benefits agreements. It failed. I then worked at 1199. I've been here for 15 years.

23 All Politics Is Local

Reflections from the Frontlines of a Progressive Electoral Movement

Maurice Mitchell

Every election is the most important election of our lifetime.

- unknown

I don't know who originally said this, but it has become so clichéd I hesitate to utter it. The 2024 election *is* arguably the most important election of our lifetime, if not for any other reason than the growing threat of the opposition. With a rising fascist movement, every election for the foreseeable future may hinge on the existential question of whether democracy lives to fight another day or we fall into the clutches of authoritarianism.

While a potential second Trump term posed a unique but clear and present danger in 2020, the conditions facing us this year may be more fraught with landmines than those we navigated at the top of the decade, when the global pandemic forced us to reckon with how we organize.

Today, we're facing a crisis of legitimacy for the very institutions we were told are the bedrock of the idea of America. People on the left and right may not agree on much, but there's near universal agreement that something is wrong. Rising international conflict, gun violence, student debt, and an affordable housing crisis are just some of the issues driving a wave of uncertainty. Even the Surgeon General, last spring, declared loneliness to be a public health crisis.

We are more networked due to technology, yet more disconnected than ever.

The old systems are dying. We see the morbid symptoms everywhere, from the aforementioned social problems to the dramatic spasms of institutional rupture like the Trump election and January 6. People are longing for connection, meaning, and answers to explain why it feels like the earth is shifting under our feet at the level of epoch-defining change.

And make no mistake, there will be change because new systems must take the place of the decaying institutions, but the direction of that change is up for grabs.

DOI: 10.4324/9781003544371-27

We have three competing visions for the ultimate prizes of hearts, minds, and governing power. One vision that calls for the crushing of dissent and the suppression of communities and cultures whose existence belies the idea of White Christian hegemony. Another vision that desires a return to the status quo and promotes a fondness for normalcy and an end to volatility, even if injustice and inequality reign.

Lastly, we have our vision that says everyone, regardless of their zip code or where they come from, should have the right to do more than just make ends meet. You should have the freedom to thrive, to dream, and to achieve. To love the people you want to love and make your own decisions about expanding your family, educating your children, or the identities that give you meaning.

It turns out that when we bring our vision to the people, they're pretty receptive.

That's the vision the Working Families Party used to lay the groundwork for a minor party takeover in Philadelphia over five years. I believe we can scale this model nationally to beat back MAGA extremists in 2024 and elect governments nationwide – on the local and state levels – that center the needs of working people.

Our view of electoral struggle began with the city council.

That governing body in the City of Brotherly Love reserves two seats for minor parties. In our two-party system, that's historically been the GOP. In a city as progressive as Philadelphia, WFP had a problem with that. No candidate, especially with one party being hijacked by MAGA extremists, should be able to sign their name on a form and waltz into the city council.

In 2018, we recruited Philly native and community organizer Kendra Brooks and Pastor Nicolas O'Rourke to run for the two at-large seats traditionally held by the minor party. We knocked on doors to establish relationships with voters everywhere and built tight relationships with the existing progressive infrastructure in the city. We brought the WFP message and the prospect of possibility to every corner of the city.

When all was said and done, Kendra triumphed at the ballot box, putting together a coalition of more than 60,000 voters who were ready for something different.

Despite the monumental win, we were not content with only winning half the battle.

All too often, political organizing is limited to GOTV. But what would happen if a people-centered party stayed around and organized month after month, year after year – before we needed people to cast a ballot? This was the question that would guide us in the years to follow.

Over the next five years, the Working Families Party built a mighty, people-powered party apparatus in Philadelphia. We'd reached out to hundreds of thousands of voters with a progressive vision for the city that included fully funded schools, fair wages, safer streets without relying on police and prisons, and so much more.

Love or loathe us, the WFP was a major player.

All that organizing work was put to the test in November 2023. Not only were we seeking to re-elect Kendra, but we were re-running Nicolas, who had returned to the community as WFP's indefatigable organizing director.

We had one massive hurdle to clear: voters get five votes for at-large city council, and convincing them to forgo a longstanding practice of giving all five of their votes to one party and walking out of the booth took a Herculean political organizing and education effort.

Politics is often a game of inches, and I believe the difference came down to what happened on Election Day. More than 500 organizers, me included, were at the polls bright and early, singing from the WFP hymnal.

Kendra jumped out to an early lead on election night and never looked back. She was coasting to reelection – and by a wider margin than her first run. After a nail-biter of a night, a final batch of reported votes put her WFP running mate, Nicolas O'Rourke, over the top. And on November 7, 2023, Philadelphia had a new "minor party:" The Working Families Party.

Philadelphia 2023 is instructive for 2024 in several key ways. We can meet voters where they are, to build genuine relationships that aren't based on the transactional "vote for me on Tuesday" style of politics that too many consultants advocate. We can co-create an agenda that puts working people at the helm of governing power, and educate the people on how we can make that agenda real.

The best time to be in the streets was yesterday; the next best time is now. Our democracy – and our very way of life – hinge on what we do with the time we have.

Onward!

24 Protecting Voter Rights

Jeff Merkley

U.S. Senator Jeff Merkley joined a Senate Committee on Rules and Administration hearing on March 12, 2024, where election officials were questioned about efforts to uphold democracy, protect voting rights, and address threats against county clerks and election workers in Oregon and nationwide. The discussions focused on safeguarding the electoral process amidst challenges and misinformation, and highlighting the importance of combating intimidation tactics aimed at undermining democratic values. The following is a transcript from that hearing,[1] reprinted with the Senator's permission.

-Editors

Senator Merkley: *Secretary Benson, you had several examples in your testimony of the intimidation of poll workers. One was an election director who was threatened to be hanged for treason, and I believe in Rochester Hills, there was a voicemail saying, "10 million patriots will surround you when you least expect it," directed toward Tina Barton. Another in Detroit City said, "you're going to pay dearly." This is all across the country and is an example of the threats that were put forward in Oregon, written on the parking lot. As you can see, that was done right after the election: "Vote don't work." (Translation: Elections don't work.) "Next time bullets." I must say I've been hearing from clerks all over my state that they're having difficulty recruiting poll workers due to these threats, which have been inspired by Trump's argument that the election was stolen. Is this happening all over the country? Secretary of State of Michigan, Jocelyn Benson: Yes, and it has since the 2020 election cycle in terms of the threats and the challenges, and my colleagues on this panel have talked about some of the solutions of anti-doxxing legislation. I think Michigan has gone a long way to pass state laws to very clearly draw a line in the sand about what is and isn't appropriate in terms of threats to election workers. I would just add one thing. One,*

DOI: 10.4324/9781003544371-28

I think the absence of any clarity from the federal government that this is not appropriate and that it is a crime to threaten an elected official in their line of official duties, I would say passing a law to clearly make it a crime. As Senator Ossoff and others have proposed, it would send a very clear message of support and protection to these individuals who have borne a lot of the brunt of the misinformation, lies, and deception that have plagued our democracy for the last several years. The other thing I'll underscore is one thing I'm particularly proud of in Michigan, where we launched the Democracy MVP program in 2020. It partners with Vote the Vet to recruit veterans. It partners with ABA nationally and in our state to recruit attorneys. What we have seen as a result also is a new generation of election workers step up to the plate determined to protect our democracy, despite the threats.

Senator Merkley: Thank you. I'm going to try and get a couple other questions here, but that is a very comprehensive answer. Thank you. And Alabama Secretary of State Wes Allen mentioned the importance of making sure that non-citizens don't vote. This has been a point of some discussion as to whether these strategies are intended to essentially intimidate people and whether this is addressing a real problem. Have you seen a significant number of non-citizens attempting to vote in your state? No. And if I recall, Michigan did some audits to try to examine that, and what did those audits find?

Secretary Benson: Yes, we take the importance of ensuring every eligible vote is counted and only eligible votes are counted very seriously. We have several layers of protection. We implemented automatic voter registration in particular to ensure documentation and also make clear to folks the consequences – legal consequences – of lying on these forms. But at the same time, we've done our work and conducted our investigations. We've consistently found that our voter rolls are clean and that non-citizens are not voting to the extent that some would allege.

Senator Merkley: So there's many ways to approach this that have worked very well, and Ms. [Janai] Nelson [Director, Legal Defense Fund], would you affirm that that is the case?

Ms. Nelson: Absolutely, there is no evidence that there are non-citizens attempting to vote in any substantial or even notable number.

Senator Merkley: Just say I hate to see people trying to address a non-problem and disguise it as a problem when they're really trying to intimidate people from voting. Miss Nelson, I wanted to turn to your testimony. As you mentioned in it, several things are done to discourage people from voting. And I've heard about these all across the country. If you have a section of the state that you don't want to vote, like a certain city, a certain poor area, a certain Native Indian Reservation, changes in polling location. You move it. You consolidate it. You proceed to open the voting place late. You proceed to understaff it so that there is a long line.

You proceed to put the voting place where there's no parking, so people get very frustrated. You proceed to run out of ballots, which is one I hadn't heard about before when you were talking about Mississippi. And so these strategies, how do we tackle these?

Ms. Nelson: Well, the way we're tackling them is we have 25 poll monitors on the ground right now in Mississippi, addressing those very issues that you just laid out. I have a real-time email from my team telling me that that's what they're seeing. There's also signage issues. There are many ways that are not easily detectable until you are in the middle of an election and voters are being disenfranchised, where there is clear targeting and a clear disregard for certain communities when they are attempting to cast a ballot. What we need, in addition to our election protection efforts, is strong legislation that will prevent some of these changes from happening without there being some preclearance – some authority that says it is okay for you to do this and it will not disproportionately harm certain voters.

Senator Merkley: I really want to just emphasize … because these things sound like legitimate operations – moving a polling location and so forth – they can be used in an extremely prejudicial manner. Thank you.

Note

1 Marcy Sutter, "Merkley Speaks with Election Officials about Threats to County Clerks and Election Workers," *Merkley* (blog), March 19, 2024, https://www.merkley.senate.gov/merkley-speaks-with-election-officials-about-threats-to-county-clerks-and-election-workers/.

Index

For Product Safety Concerns and Information please contact our EU
representative GPSR@taylorandfrancis.com
Taylor & Francis Verlag GmbH, Kaufingerstraße 24, 80331 München, Germany

www.ingramcontent.com/pod-product-compliance
Lightning Source LLC
Chambersburg PA
CBHW050532270326
41926CB00015B/3180